MONAST
VOCATION

❖

ROWAN WILLIAMS

SISTERS OF THE
LOVE OF GOD

❖

FAIRACRES PUBLICATIONS 200

SLG PRESS
Oxford

© 2021 SLG Press
First Edition 2021

Fairacres Publications No. 200

Print ISBN 978-0-7283-0308-9
Fairacres Publications Series ISSN 0307-1405

Paul Monk asserts his right under the Copyright, Designs and Patents Act 1988, to be identified as the author of the Preface of this work.
Rowan Williams asserts his right under the Copyright, Designs and Patents Act 1988, to be identified as the author of the chapter: 'The Call to Love' of this work. The Sisters of the Love of God assert their right under the Copyright, Designs and Patents Act 1988, to be identified as the authors of the chapters: 'Poverty', 'Chastity', 'Obedience', 'Contemplation and Enclosure', 'The Cell' and 'Journey' in this work.

The publishers have no control over, or responsibility for, any third-party website referred to or in this book. All internet addresses given in the this book were correct at the time of going to press. The author and publisher regret any inconvenience caused if addresses have changed or sites have ceased to exist, but can accept no responsibility for any such changes.

Biblical quotations are taken from the New Revised Standard Version except for 'Poverty', in which the quotations are taken from the Revised English Bible.

Edited and typeset in Palatino Linotype by Julia Craig-McFeely

SLG Press
Convent of the Incarnation
Fairacres • Oxford
www.slgpress.co.uk

Printed by
Grosvenor Group Ltd, Loughton, Essex

MONASTIC
VOCATION

ACKNOWLEDGEMENTS

'Preface': Adapted from a homily preached on the Feast of St Dunstan at St Barnabas Church, Clarksfield, Oldham.

'The Call to Love': first published as *Vocations* by Rowan Williams, originally an address given to theological students at Westcott House, first appeared in print in *Encounter and Exchange*, and was subsequently reprinted by the Vocations Team of the Society of St Francis. Reprinted with permission.

'Contemplation and Enclosure': A paper read at the conference on Modern Spirituality at the Royal Foundation of St Katherine, Stepney, in February 1971, Published in *Fairacres Chronicle* Vol. 4, No. 1 (March 1971), then as *Contemplation and Enclosure*, Fairacres Pamphlet No. 18, 1971.

'Journey' by Sr Rosemary SLG first printed in *Anglican Religious Life Yearbook* 2014–2015 © Canterbury Press. Used by permission rights@hymnsam.co.uk.

CONTENTS

—◆—

—◆—

THE CALL

The last rose unfurls
and dances in the wind,
out of step and out of sight
from her sisters, from her friends.

A late bloomer, all alone,
so who is there to know
how she lifts her face up,
arms outstretched just so?

yet she is seen by one
whom she cannot see,
and he whispers in the wind,
come and dance with me.

SR STEPHANIE-THÉRÈSE SLG

Preface

The word vocation comes from the Latin 'vocatio' that means 'the call'. We get words like 'vocal' from the same root. From within a Christian context, we truly follow a vocation when we hear the call of God in our lives ... and obey it.

The idea of a Christian vocation goes something like this: God wants us to serve Him to the uttermost. God can work through us in proportion that we live Godly lives. To ensure our lives are indeed Godly, He equips us by giving us His Holy Spirit. We receive the Holy Spirit at baptism and further enable the Spirit's action through all the usual Christian graces of prayer and meditation, charity and obedience, and the sacraments. That way we are better equipped to hear when the Spirit calls us.

As we listen to the Spirit in our soul, the Spirit directs us to the people, places and tasks that God wants. We might imagine that God programs (like a computer) to work in a particular way, but a disciple is never robotic or mindless. Even if we listen intently, we still have free will: we have choices such as whether to obey, and how. God is love (1 John 4:16) and love could not operate otherwise.

As we try to live out our Christian vocation we operate in the times and places where love intersects with action. We therefore anticipate the Holy Spirit prompting us to love as Jesus would love but in the places God has chosen for our love to operate. It is tempting here to remember the saying of St John of the Cross, 'Where there is no love, put love—and you will find love.' Viewed in these ways, our vocation is to love as Jesus loved us. The New Commandment becomes simply a way of telling us who God wants us to be. He wants us to be people of love.

This can sound quite theoretical. It isn't. It is simply saying that the vocation of every sincere Christian is to love as Jesus did. Hence this current work. To that end, the thoughts printed here each look at an aspect of monastic vocation: it is the call of God, a call to love, a call into life. It is God's call to us of a life loved for and in Him.

PAUL MONK

1

THE CALL TO LOVE
The Right Revd Rowan Williams

The trouble with the idea of vocation is that most of us, if we are honest, have a rather dramatic idea of it. I do not mean *dramatic* just in the sense of *self-dramatizing*, but *dramatic* in the simpler sense of *theatrical*—vocation as *casting*, you might say. God has a purpose for the world, a very long and very good play, even longer and better than Shaw's *Back to Methuselah*, with plenty of juicy parts in it. The nuisance is that He draws up the cast-list before doing any auditions: each of us finds himself or herself *called* to fulfil a definite role; but we have not actually seen the script, and as time goes on we may suspect we should do better in another part. We think we could play Hamlet very effectively if only our talents were not so successfully concealed by the fact that we have a two-minute appearance as Second Grave-digger. Or else we find the burden of learning all the lines for Claudius rather too much and think we prefer an impressive walk-on part like Fortinbras. What I mean is that this not-uncommon way of talking about vocation as God finding us a *part to play* is actually rather problematic: there will always be the danger of a suspicion that we are not *really* being used, stretched, and so on, and a flicker of resentment at being consigned to undue prominence or unjust obscurity. In short, we are uneasy about the hint of arbitrariness in all this.

I Hear—and I Obey?

It is quite true that this kind of language has deep roots in our faith. There is Isaiah's call: the King says, *Whom shall I send?* the prophet says, *Send me.* There is a task to be performed; it is offered, who may dare refuse? There are souls like Jeremiah and Paul, set apart from before birth for the work of God, writhing and crying under the terrible, merciless pressure of their burden, unable to ignore their calling—'If I say, "I will not mention Him, or speak any more His name", there is in my heart as it were a burning fire shut up in my bones, and I am weary with holding it in, and I cannot.' (Jer. 20:9)—

3

and yet tortured and almost destroyed by it. There are those who try to escape: Herbert's great poems of revolt ('I struck the board and cry'd, No more'[1]), or Hopkins' sonnets testify to the passion to get away from the unbearable pain of uselessness, loneliness and frustration. Or think of the *Curé d'Ars* trying again and again to run away to a monastery to get away from the relentless crowds of penitents, and always being prevented. Vocation here is indeed a dreadful falling into the hands of the living God, being bound upon a wheel of fire. God has decided; you may struggle or revolt, but here is this clear will, to be done whatever the cost. All I am asked for is compliance: in a real sense, I have no *rights* here. I obey, I bear the crucifying consequences, because I have, however dimly and weakly, chosen to love God and to do His will, chosen to see that as the one ultimately, unconditionally worthwhile thing a human being can do. It may seem arbitrary; but the clay does not argue with the potter; behind it all is the unimaginable promise just glimpsed—'Methought I heard one calling, child';[2] treasure in heaven; the hundred-fold recompense of God's fatherly acceptance.

All of that is, I believe, quite genuinely central to the Christian doctrine of vocation, but there is a lot that it does not say. On this, pattern, the will of God is seen as still being something very like the preferences of God: God would like so-and-so to be a priest or a nun or something, and so that is what so-and-so must be. Once again, if there is a complaint about arbitrariness, the answer is ready to hand that God's ways are not ours. 'Why does X have to be a nun? What a marvellous wife and mother she would have made!' But God is inscrutable, and He has decreed frustration for X on one level, for the sake of greater fruitfulness on another. He chooses where He wills: there is no set of conditions for His grace. We are to rejoice in the fact that, weak and sinful and silly as we are, God has chosen us for the privilege of loving and serving Him. Grace upon grace: how wonderful that God is arbitrary—at least for those of us who are chosen. There is a bit of a problem about the rest.

---

[1] George Herbert, 'The Collar'.
[2] Ibid.

4

God's Creative Word

Grace upon grace; but what about nature? Does grace necessarily interrupt and overturn and deny and frustrate? Is it not supposed to fulfil? Once put in terms like this the question, and the dimensions of the problem, become clear and very alarming—grace and nature, creation and redemption, election and reprobation—inescapable and horribly complex matters. In the long run, we cannot think usefully about vocation without some thinking about these wider things.

It is very important, for instance, to remember that in the Old Testament *calling* and *creating* are closely associated. Look at Is. 40:26—God creating the stars and calling them by name—and the echoes of that in the psalter. Think too of the image of God creating and recreating human beings by *naming* them. God, say the prophets and poets of Israel, has called you by name. As at first, when Jacob wrestled with the angel, God calls, consecrates to His service, by giving a name. Though there is nothing specific in the New Testament that says we should, we still reflect this sense by associating baptism, God's grace calling people into Christ, with the giving of a name. As the Greek Fathers liked to say, God creates by uttering a multitude of *logoi* designating words, names: creation springs into being in order to *answer* God's speech, God's call, so that His Word does not return to Him empty (Is. 55:11). So in the most basic sense of all, God's call is the call to *be:* the *vocation* of creatures is to exist. Secondly, the vocation of creatures is to exist *as themselves,* to be bearers of their names, answering to the word that gives each its distinctive identity. The act of creation can be seen as quite simply this: the vocation of things to be themselves, distinctive, spare and strange. God does not first create and then differentiate a great multitude of roles within creation: in one act He creates a multiple, noisy, jostling and diverse reality.

Called from Eternity

So with the human world. God does not create human ciphers, a pool of cheap labour to whom jobs can be assigned at will. Each human being called into existence by Him exists as a distinct part of a great interlocking web of identities. Each is a unique point in this great net.

5

To be *is* to be where you are, who you are, and what you are—a person with certain genetic composition, a certain social status, a certain set of capabilities. From the moment of birth (even from before that) onwards, you will be at each moment that particular bundle of conditioning and possibilities. To talk about God as your creator means to recognise at each moment that it is His desire for you to be, and so His desire for you to be there as the person you are. It means He is calling you by your name, at each and every moment, wanting you to be you.

This may be the clue to the problems we have in thinking of vocation. It is not that God looks down from heaven at a certain moment and just drops a vocation on us, as if He were utterly uninterested and uninvolved in what is actually there. If we take seriously the idea that God is faithful and does not change, we need to think of Him speaking over and over again the *same* word to us—our true name, our real identity—and making us be, over and over again, in that speech of His, in His Word. In other words: vocation does not happen, once and for all, at a fixed date. Paul himself, who seems to be the classic instance to the contrary, recognizes this precisely in talking about being set apart *from His mother's womb*. It happens from birth to death; and what we usually call 'vocation' is only a name for the moment of crisis within the unbroken process.

Hidden in God

A moment of crisis: because answering the call to be oneself at any given moment is not at all easy. In spite of what it may sound like, it is not a bland acceptance of the *status quo* in your life, or a licence to surrender to every possible impulse. God asks for His Word to be answered, He asks response. To exist really is to exist as responding-to-God. Each of us is called to *be* a different kind of response to God, to mirror God in unique ways, show God what we are like, so to speak, from innumerable new and different standpoints.

So one clue to our identity is this, the idea of *mirroring* God: we have to find what is our particular way of *playing back* to God His self-sharing, self-losing care and compassion, the love because of which He speaks and calls in the first place.

6

To Become My True Self

Crises occur at those points where we see how unreality, our selfish, self-protecting illusions, our struggles for cheap security, block the way to our answering the call to be. To live like this, to nurture and develop this image of myself, may be safe, but it is not true: insofar as it is unreal it is un-Godly. God cannot reach me if I am not there.

So the crisis comes when we put the questions, 'What am I denying, what am I refusing to see in myself? What am I trying to avoid?' This is where we have to begin really to attend, to ourselves and to the world around, to find out what is true and what is false in us. Not just introspection, because we do not just live in private selves: we have to reckon with the needs and expectations of others, with the practical realities of life, society and family and so on; not just collusion with those needs, because we have our own secrets of memory, and temperament, and desire. We have to listen harder than ever—to each other and to our own hearts. What emerges is, perhaps, that sense of near-inevitability, that obscurely authoritative impulse that crystallizes for some as 'a vocation', the sense that being myself will demand of me a certain kind of commitment. The process can be rapid or slow, it can work at a conscious or a subconscious level with or without a single recognizable point of decision; but this is, I think, the basis of what goes on.

Accepting Who I Am

Those whose job it is to assess the reality or adequacy of *vocations* can really do no more than attempt to say, have you reckoned with *that* aspect of yourself? With *that* feature of your relationships? Is this actually *you* we have got here? Or is it another defence, another game?

That is one reason why it is so important to have some kind of shared life bound up with vocational training. None of us, I imagine, can discover the truth from the perspective of an isolated individual existence. Our hearts are infinitely cunning in self-deceit: we need others to let the cold light of accuracy shine on our evasions and posturings. All of us have to ask one another, *Tell me who you think I am* at times; and all of us are obliged to answer that with as much candour— and as much charity—as we can. Someone's life depends on it.

It is all a way of restating the idea that vocation has to do with *saving your soul*—not by acquiring a secure position of holiness, but by learning to shed the unreality that simply suffocates the very life of the soul.

It has to do with recognizing that my relation with God (and so with everybody) depends absolutely on making the decision to be what I am, to answer God's Word; and doing this without fuss and existentialist drama because what I am is already known and loved and accepted in God. As Karl Barth loved to say, 'God has chosen us all in Christ: at the deepest level we are all called Jesus in the eyes of the Father ('Methought I thought I heard one calling, *Child!* ...').[3] Sometimes this will look and feel arbitrary. There will be few continuities, no readily graspable pattern in it all, the crisis will be severe and shattering. That is a measure not of God's whimsical and capricious despotism, but of how far I have really been from myself (Augustine's *Confessions* have some wonderful things to say about this).

The Cost of Reality

I may rage and cry at the frustrations of my calling and yet know— like Herbert, Hopkins, Jean Vianney, Jeremiah, and all the others—know beyond doubt that while this may be dreadful, any-thing else would be worse; an invention, a game.

Here at least, whatever the cost, I am *in the truth.* The nun may say (as I have heard nuns say), "I *know* I would be a wonderful wife and mother. I know I have it in me to live that out successfully and happily, that it answers to a great area of my temperament, but knowing that does not make things easier. I know too that for me that would be playing, messing around with a tame reality I could control; and reality is not like that." Vocation is, you could say, what is left when all the games have stopped. It is that elusive residue that we are here to discover, and to help one another to discover.

---

[3] Herbert, 'The Collar'.

A story to conclude:

Rabbi Yehuda Loew ben Bezalel was the greatest rabbi of his age in Europe, the man who, in his house in Prague, created the Golem, the animated form of a man, to which he gave life by putting under its tongue a slip of paper bearing the Unutterable Name of God. One night, Rabbi Yehuda had a dream: he dreamt that he had died and was brought before the Throne. And the angel who stands before the Throne said to him: "Who are you?" "I am Rabbi Yehuda of Prague, the maker of the Golem", he replied, "Tell me, my lord, if my name is written in the book of the names of those who will have a share in the kingdom." "Wait here", said the angel; "I shall read the names of all those who have died today that are written in the Book." And he read the names, thousands of them, strange names to the ears of Rabbi Yehuda; as the angel read, the rabbi saw the spirits of those whose names had been called fly into the glory that sat above the Throne. At last he finished reading, and Rabbi Yehuda's name had not been called, and he wept bitterly and cried out against the angel. And the angel said, "I have called your name." Rabbi Yehuda said, "I did not hear it", and the angel said: "In the Book are written the names of all men and women who have ever lived on the earth, for every soul is an inheritor of the kingdom. But many come here who have never heard their true names on the lips of man or angel. They have lived believing that they know their names; and so when they are called to their share in the kingdom, they do not hear their names as their own. They do not recognise that it is for them that the gates of the kingdom are opened. So they must wait here until they hear their names and know them. Perhaps in their lifetime one man or woman has once called them by their right name: here they shall stay until they have remembered. Perhaps no one ever has called them by their right name: here they shall stay till they are silent enough to hear the King of the Universe Himself calling them."

At this, Rabbi Yehuda woke, and, rising from his bed with tears, he covered his head and lay prostrate on the ground, and prayed: "Master of the Universe! Grant me once before I die to hear my own true name on the lips of my brothers."

The *SLG Rule* and *SLG Way of Life* referred to below are available on the SLG website: www.slg.org.uk/who-we-are/the-rule

POVERTY

Sr Susan SLG

*The troubles they have been through have tried them hard,
yet in all this they have been so exuberantly happy that from
the depths of their poverty they have shown themselves lavishly
open-handed.* (2 Cor. 8:2)

*You know the generosity of our Lord Jesus Christ:
He was rich, yet for your sakes He became poor, so that through
His poverty you might become rich.* (2 Cor. 8:9)[1]

The Word 'Poverty'

In our world of nearly instant communication, when we can see, day
by day, the manner in which people throughout the world are forced
to live: in refugee camps, in situations of catastrophic flooding or
other natural disaster, or indeed just as their ordinary day-to-day
existence, the word poverty has perhaps become synonymous with
destitution. In the UK politicians speak about 'bringing children out
of poverty', and there was the 'Say No to Poverty' movement. In the
face of this we could conclude that most monks and nuns who take
a Vow of Poverty and live in community do not live in poverty at all,
and that it is an inappropriate word to express what they desire to
communicate. And yet there are other interpretations.

I will look briefly at some of them from the Bible and from the
Rules of three religious/monastic communities/orders. I will hope to
evaluate poverty in the light of the experience of those of us (monks
and nuns) who are trying to live it now in the West.

The Bible: Old Testament

There is a great deal in the Old Testament about 'the poor'. There
are the impressive bits about not picking up a fallen sheaf when you
are harvesting, and leaving the verges of your fields for the poor
(Lev. 23:22), from which we can conclude that there was a level of

---

[1] Scriptural quotations in this chapter are taken from the Revised English Bible.

concern or care for the poor. It went hand in hand, however, with the practice of extorting surplus crops from them. We are forced to wonder if the charitable acts were simply a way of keeping the poor alive in order that they might serve the wealthy: 'While appropriating peasant surpluses to fund bureaucracy, building projects, wars, and expensive lifestyles, the dominant consuming class usually allowed the producing class just enough surplus to keep it at subsistence level'.[2] It would seem fair to conclude that if you could get out of poverty you would, but you would also aim to keep poor people poor to enable your lifestyle. And we could ask if that is still true today.

In the Bible, in both the New Testament and the Old, the word 'poverty' is used much less frequently than the descriptive word 'poor'. This must be because the Bible is much less interested in abstract states than in the actual people who rejoice in or suffer from them. However 'poverty' does appear, as for instance, when Joseph, Pharaoh's right-hand man in Egypt and in charge of the distribution of grain, says to his brothers, 'I shall see that you and your household … are not reduced to poverty' (Gen. 45:10–11). Poverty in this case would have been induced by a long drought and resulted ultimately in death. That is a meaning of poverty we are familiar with via the media. The book of Proverbs, though, gives insights of a rather different nature. The author writes about the dangers and the blessings of both extreme poverty and great wealth, and then ends his work with a prayer to God proclaiming a possible middle way:

> Two things I ask of you—
> do not withhold them in my lifetime:
> put fraud and lying far from me;
> give me neither poverty nor wealth,
> but provide me with the food I need,
> for if I have too much I shall deny you
> and say 'who is the Lord?'
> and if I am reduced to poverty I shall steal
> and besmirch the name of my God' (Prov. 30:7–9).

---

[2] Gale A. Yee, 'The Creation of Poverty in Ancient Israel', *Supplement Series for the Journal of Religion and Society,* 10 (2014), 4–19.

The author is concerned with our moral or spiritual well-being; extreme poverty is to be avoided, but so is excessive wealth.

The Bible: New Testament

When we come to the New Testament there is a different message. On the one hand poverty is something that it is a duty of the followers of Christ to alleviate, and on the other it is a way of life to copy, for Jesus himself seems to have lived in, at least relative, poverty.

Most people with some knowledge of the Bible would, I think, go first to the Beatitudes if looking for the teaching of Jesus: 'Blessed are the poor in spirit, for theirs is the kingdom of heaven' in Matt. 5:3, or even more starkly in Luke 6:20, 'Blessed are those who are in need; the kingdom of God is yours'. These sayings must be fundamental to all Christian living and yet what do they mean? The first edition of the New English Bible produced a paraphrase for 'poor in spirit': the translators wrote 'blessed are those who know their need of God', something that applies to all, rich and poor, and is an understanding of poverty that will certainly resonate for those under religious or monastic vows.

What about Jesus himself though? The only saying that I can remember in which He may refer to his personal circumstances is His response to a, perhaps idealistic, follower: 'foxes have their holes and the birds of the air have their roosts; but the Son of Man has nowhere to lay His head' (Matt. 8:20). Maybe once He had left His parents' house in Nazareth Jesus did not have a home of His own. It is possible. Certainly we see Him constantly on the move, accepting meals from friends and critics alike, and Matthew 27:55 seems to indicate that a group of women took care of Him and His disciples, although what form this care took is not clear. The conclusion, perhaps, is that He lived day by day, 'in the present moment'. Possibly, though, His domestic circumstances were not the important thing, but rather what we might call the poverty of His very being as we see it in St Paul's letter to the Philippians: 'He did not count equality with God a thing to be grasped, but emptied himself ... ' (Phil. 2:6–7), and 'He was rich, yet for your sake He became poor' (2 Cor. 8:9).

'Emptied himself' would seem to indicate a poverty of being beyond our imaginations. We can perhaps learn a little more from the way Jesus's followers lived after His death.

The positive and negative experiences of poverty are underlined in the letters to the churches in the book of Revelation. The author writes to the church in Smyrna, 'I know how hard-pressed and poor you are, but in reality you are rich' (Rev. 2:9). And to the church in Laodicea: 'You say, "How rich I am! What a fortune I have made! I have everything I want." In fact, though you do not realise it, you are a pitiful wretch, poor, blind and naked' (Rev. 3:17). These two statements are, in their way, an illustration of what the author of Proverbs was trying to convey. There are two experiences of poverty: one a blessing and one definitely not. The book of Revelation is thought to have been written at the end of the first century or early in the second, so the conviction of the possible blessing of poverty had remained through into at least the second or third generation of Christians. What it meant, in one respect anyway, is illustrated in the Acts when the author describes the attitude of the followers of Jesus to property and ownership: 'The whole company of believers was united in heart and soul. Not one of them claimed any of his possessions as his own; everything was held in common.' The author goes on to state that no one among them was ever needy, as those who had property or land would sell it so that the proceeds could be distributed to whoever had need (Acts 4:32–7). This is at the heart of religious/monastic poverty, and is taken up into many community rules. But it is not, of course, the only text that has been influential in the adoption of poverty. There is also the story of the rich (young) man whom Jesus told to go and sell all his possessions and give the proceeds to the poor (Matt. 19:21). It was hearing this that influenced St Antony the Great who was traditionally the first monk. Francis of Assisi was similarly moved to action on hearing the story of the commissioning of the twelve: 'take no gold, silver or copper, no pack for the road, no second coat, no sandals, no stick' (Matt. 10:9–10). This resulted in the establishment of groups of both men and women committed to the life of wandering poor. These passages must have been influential more widely too, but they are not taken up into the three Rules that I will look at, two of which were written for groups of men and women living in community, and one for friars.

Ancient Rules

One of the earliest of the Ancient Rules (the earliest in the West) is that of Augustine of Hippo, written about 397 AD, followed by that of St Benedict early in the sixth century. The Carmelite and Franciscan Orders both emerged in the twelfth to thirteenth centuries, and in both the men were 'friars', that is members of mendicant orders. The women however, because of the custom of the time, were enclosed. St Francis and his followers are particularly known for their poverty, but I have chosen the Rule of St Albert because he wrote the Carmelite Rule for the newly-founded Carmelite Order between 1206 and 1214 and the community to which I belong was founded with the Carmelite way of life in mind and so it is the one I know best from experience.

Augustine begins with the Acts text and makes two points: one that brothers or sisters should be 'one in mind and heart', the other that no one should possess anything as their own. It is clear from the way he makes the points that the one depends on the other, but whether the physical sharing of goods comes first and helps the community members to be of one mind and heart, or whether growth in mutual love results in the sharing, is not clear to me. It may well be that it is a process of growing in both: sometimes one taking precedence, sometimes the other. Today this dispossession may take place either before entering a community, or at the point of making the commitment for life by taking Life Vows, or often a combination of both. Augustine's stance is clear: 'Those who owned possessions in the world should readily agree that, from the moment they enter the religious life, these things become the property of the community.'[3] It does not mean you will not have what you need, but it will not be your own—whether it is clothes, books or the things you require for the work you are assigned. However, Augustine recognizes that putting this into practice requires

---

[3] Augustine, *Rule* 1:2. The translation I have used is T. Van Bavel, *The Rule of St Augustine* (London: DLT, 1984).

some flexibility; people have different strengths and needs. And so he allows for differences in background and physical capacity but also puts in place some teaching about the possible pitfalls. He warns against pride, for instance, when he writes about members of the community who have come from wealthy families: 'The fact that they have made some of their possessions available to the community gives them no reason to have a high opinion of themselves'.[4] And with regard to envy that can so easily creep in, 'There are some who are weaker because of their former manner of life. If an exception is made for them at table, those who are stronger because they have come from a different way of life ought not to take it amiss or to consider it unfair.'[5] The reason for this he expresses at the end of the first chapter: 'You are all to live together, therefore, in one mind and one heart, and honour God in one another because each of you has become His temple.'[6]

Benedictines do not take a Vow of Poverty, or of Chastity, instead they take a vow to *Conversatio Morum*. This is a vow to a daily reshaping of the mind and heart. It includes personal poverty and communal simplicity of life. In his Rule Benedict takes up the same emphasis as Augustine, writing about the need for letting go of personal property in order that 'all the members are to be at peace'[7] and he enlarges it a little in Chapters 54 and 55. In the latter it is stipulated that the clothes supplied from the common wardrobe are to be allocated by the abbot and should be adequate. In this way the monk will have no need to look elsewhere and, like Augustine the abbot takes into account not only the climate and the work, but the possible weaknesses and needs of individual brothers. He too is aware of the danger of envy and guards against it as much as possible.

St Albert, in the Rule he established for the Carmelite Friars in the twelfth century, writes, 'None of the brethren is to claim something as

---

[4] Augustine, *Rule* 1:7.

[5] Augustine, *Rule* 3:3.

[6] Augustine, *Rule* 1:8. Cf. 2 Cor. 6:16: 'For we are the temple of the living God'.

[7] *Rule of St Benedict* 34:5, For St Benedict's Rule the translation and edition I have used is by Timothy Fry OSB, *The Rule of St Benedict* (Collegeville MN: Liturgical Press, 1980).

his own; everything is to be in common, and is to be distributed to each one by the Prior ... having regard to the age and needs of each one'.[8]

All three Rules have withstood the test of time and proved themselves capable of interpretation in the modern world so that they truly are, for those who try to live by them, a means of giving oneself to God.

Today

In terms of material possessions people's experiences vary hugely of course, both in how much they possess and how they feel about disposing of it; but the primary thing we leave, whatever our material situation, is our family and friends. You have to let go and hold fast to the belief that God has called you to pray for them rather than to be with them physically. Even with the relaxation of enclosure I think the wrench must still be there because you are going somewhere they cannot follow, or only very peripherally.

Then, as time goes by you find that you have to deal externally with things, and you are asked to make your final disposition of all the possessions you had acquired before entering. After that we try to have nothing except what is provided for our use. To some people the external things, what we are given to wear or use, may seem less important than the internal response. That can be true, but only, I think, if we have become sufficiently detached not to mind if we have them or not. It is very easy to collect things, both corporately and individually, 'in case they might be useful', or simply because it has been given to you. I was struck when, a long time ago, I read an article by Antony Bloom about his life as a monk. He had given up everything only to find himself holding on tight to a stub of a pencil. For us in the twenty-first century it is not likely to be a pencil, but the chances are we are holding onto something from which we have to let go. It could be a physical object that is likely to have emotions attached to it, or habits, once helpful but

---

[8] Christopher O'Donnell O. CARM, trans., *Rule of Albert as Approved by Innocent IV (1247)*, 12 [IX/x], , unpublished revised translation, 2002; online version at http://www.carmelites.ie/Rule.pdf, page 4 (accessed 17 May 2021).

now getting in the way. Yet in the midst of all this dispossession the Gospel records Jesus as saying, 'there is no one who has given up home, or wife, brothers, parents or children, for the sake of the king-dom of God, who will not be repaid many times over in this age, and in the age to come have eternal life' (Luke 18:29–30). I do not know about eternal life, I do know that we re-establish most rela-tionships we have had, and make new ones, but the leaving of people and things has to happen, and it is a life-long condition requiring vigilance and the ability to admit that we have fallen into acquisitiveness yet again. But, even with the frailties we all experi-ence, 'not to have' is liberating.

Among the things that may be taken from us, or seem to be in the beginning anyway, are the aptitudes we are born with, and the skills and training we acquired as we became adults. We each work in the community where we are needed, and we learn that success is not our goal. As time goes on our experience and skills may be used, but not necessarily; each individual has committed her whole life to God through the community. An unexpected outcome of this, however, may be the development of completely unexpected skills, and the discovery of enjoyment in whatever we are given to do. The leaving has to happen first though. This, because it is so personal to our being, may make us ask 'who am I?'.

This interior experience of poverty is more difficult to write about. It may be an experience of a loss of identity and the gradual finding of a new one, but it will also be a sense of inadequacy, of re-peated failure. Anyone would think that this is, surely, a depressing experience, undermining self-confidence? Yes and no. Our own *Way of Life* document gives us the aim:

> … we seek to stand still before God in our naked humanity. When we have exhausted all our own resources, we have nothing left but to turn to God, to rely on His strength.[9]

It would seem that we have to find ourselves at the bottom in order to rely on God. There are various things that can help us: the detachment

---

[9] 'Poverty' in *SLG Way of Life*, 19.

from possessions which we have looked at is one, but now we must extend it to a detachment from our own ideas of what is good and necessary so that 'God can fill the space'. That last statement is the purpose of it all. It does not happen completely in this life but with faithfulness and perseverance it will start to happen. As Augustine says, God will fill our wineskin, our bag, according to our capacity.[10] There are helpers on the journey, of course, none of us is alone. The chief of these are our Sisters and Brothers: 'Gradually we learn to accept and to forgive each other, aware that we are loved just as we are and that we have nothing we have not been given'.[11]

Our Brothers and Sisters come to the fore in another context: that of poverty of choice. We can probably manage, for instance, the clothing and the lack of choice implied in wearing a habit, but we had been prepared for that. We are not, on the ÷whole, prepared for implications inherent in the lack of choice about whom we will live with. Again people differ in their response, but for everyone there will undoubtedly be difficulties. However if we have not chosen our companions ourselves, God clearly has, and we learn to live with them and indeed to rejoice in them. There will be things about other people that we will never understand and it is a case of learning to live positively with difference.

All of this, however, has no value in itself, it is only positive if it is a way of opening ourselves up, or emptying ourselves out, to God; if it is about recognizing that Christ is present in the other person. It is about each individual person's focus, and about love. If we can become detached from possessions and people, while still valuing them, we are making the space I referred to. It is space for God, but also for other people. St Teresa of Avila teaches that whatever gift of prayer we receive, if it is truly from God, it will result in service of others. The freedom that I have claimed comes with dispossession and detachment is enjoyed by each person, but it is not just for oneself. Jesus says, "You did not choose me but I chose you" (John 15:16), and He chooses us for service in a life of prayer that in

---

[10] Augustine, Homily 4:6 on the First Letter of John.
[11] 'Poverty' in SLG *Way of Life*, 19.

turn spills over into action. The quotation continues, 'I appointed you to go and bear fruit, fruit that will last'.

All I have written applies in some sense to every Christian person, though applied differently. For Augustine 'a monastery was simply that place where that fire of love was given a chance to burn more vividly than elsewhere'.[12] Or as John Cassian puts it:

> ... perfection is not immediately arrived at by being stripped and deprived of all one's wealth, or by giving up one's honours, unless there is that love whose elements the Apostle [Paul] describes, which consists in purity of heart alone.[13]

———◆———

---

[12] Peter Brown, *Through the Eye of a Needle* (Princeton: Princeton University Press, 2012), 177.

[13] John Cassian, *Conferences*, conference 1 chapter 6, trans. and ed. Boniface Ramsey OP, *John Cassian: The Conferences*, Ancient Christian Writers, 57 (New York: Newman Press, 1997), 45.

THE VOW OF CHASTITY
Sr Clare-Louise SLG

When the reason behind living the vows is changed from a focus solely on the moral and ethical (important as they are), to the spiritual and the social, a different emphasis and understanding emerges. All the vows are much more than mere prohibitions or limitations that feel death-dealing rather than life-affirming; rather they help to lead the individual towards the state of purity of heart, that, as the Beatitudes promise, leads us to see God. The vows are a way of redirecting the whole person towards God. As the *SLG Rule* puts it:

> Profession under the monastic Vows re-directs to God the natural life of men and women in their ownership of things, in the exercise of all creative powers, and in the complete control of all self-interest.[1]

As with the other vows, we need to ask first, what is the Vow of Chastity aiming for? What is its intention? It is always a danger that the vows will be viewed merely as a list of *don'ts* – 'Poverty, chastity and obedience: no stuff, no sex, no freedom!' Chastity can be the vow where this misunderstanding of mere prohibition can be especially difficult to address. With the other vows, especially the Vow of Poverty, we may be able to understand the vow within a larger environmental and ethical context. The slogan coined by Mahatma Gandhi, *live simply, that others may simply live*, illustrates this. With the Vow of Chastity, the common belief is that it has all to do with not having sex. Many may simply see it as a waste of a life, and a particularly cold and loveless one at that. The 'sexually-repressed spinster' archetype.

The reason for all the vows is to free and re-direct the human person to create the space to allow a deeper and more heartfelt love for God and for His creation. While obedience enables us to listen to the true needs of circumstances and to respond in a prayerful manner,

---

[1] *SLG Rule*, ch. 1 'The Monastic State'.

and poverty teaches us to rely only on God, chastity is designed to free us up for love. A marvellous passage, gathered from the writings of St Ælred of Rievaulx (1110–1167) by Esther de Waal, illustrates this:

> That a person may love himself,
> the love of God is formed in him;
> that one may love one's neighbour,
> the capacity of one's heart is enlarged.
> Then as the divine fire grows warmer
> little by little
> it wondrously absorbs the other loves into its fulness,
> like so many sparks.
> And so it leads all the soul's love with it
> to that supreme and ineffable good
> where neither self nor neighbour is loved for self or neighbour
> but only insofar as each fades away from self
> and is borne totally into God.
> Meanwhile, these three loves
> are engendered by one another,
> nourished by one another,
> and fanned into flame by one another.
> Then they are all brought into perfection together.[2]

In this passage St Ælred suggests that the practice of chastity enables the enlarging of the heart to allow a greater love of both God and neighbour than might otherwise be possible:

> That a person may love himself,
> the love of God is formed in him;
> that one may love one's neighbour,
> the capacity of one's heart is enlarged.

It is interesting to note that St Ælred *begins* with a person's love for himself: to love another, whether divine or human, it is first necessary that we love ourselves rightly. Disordered self-love, whether revealed by self-neglect or self-obsession, prevents us from being in a right relationship with another. At the same time, in a

---

[2] Translation cited in Esther de Waal, *The Way of Simplicity: The Cistercian Tradition* (Maryknoll NY: Orbis, 1998), 147.

chicken-and-egg conundrum of which comes first, in order to love oneself correctly the love of God must be formed in us; one aspect of the practice of the vows is that it opens our hearts to a right relationship with God. Once we are in a right relationship both with God and with ourselves our hearts are enlarged to be in a right relationship with others.

In our own inner experience of our lives as Christians, this can often be a tricky path to navigate. Christianity has been misunderstood as promoting a negative view of the body and a misplaced sense of guilt and lack of self-worth in individuals. Phrases such as 'sinful flesh' have been seen as the opposite of 'spiritual things' with the resulting development of a dichotomy between body and spirit: body equals bad, spirit equals good in this way of looking at things. At its worst we may see ourselves as 'miserable sinners', not worthy of love in the sight of God. The Vow of Chastity has been used to hide or legitimize a false and repressed view of sexuality in general and of women's sexuality in particular.

The scriptural use of the phrase 'sinful flesh', for example in some of the Letters of St Paul, can easily seem to support this misunderstanding. At first glance Paul seems to have a low opinion of the flesh as that which is sinful and in conflict with the Spirit. Rather, however, Paul wants to impress on his readers that what matters is what controls or influences our actions:

> For those who live according to the flesh set their minds on the things of the flesh, but those who live according to the Spirit set their minds on the things of the Spirit. To set the mind on the flesh is death, but to set the mind on the Spirit is life and peace.
>
> (Rom. 8:5–6)

The body as such is not evil, but if distorted desires rather than God's Spirit dominate our existence, we can readily fall into false and harmful forms of desire and action. The flesh in Scripture is something that is not inherently evil; it signifies that which is merely human rather than that which is empowered by God's Spirit.

In our world today we see this negative dichotomy echoed in the world of beauty and of advertising, when a particular look is valued over others and people can find themselves shamed because of their weight, their skin colour, or because of a disability. Women and men struggle to reach a desired appearance leading to eating disorders, depression and despair. In the same way our relationships with each other can be distorted when they exist only to meet our own perceived needs and not as a relationship between two individuals, precious in the eyes of God. If we feel empty, alone and unsafe we will tend to seek comfort and validation in others. When we can find our identity and security in love of God and in a healthy sense of self-worth based on that relationship, then we will be able to meet others with freedom and openness.

The saints and teachers of the early Church were aware that the human person could be influenced negatively by distorted passions and desires. John Cassian, and his teacher Evagrius, developed a whole understanding of the way in which uncontrolled thoughts could lead to passions, that in their turn led to potentially sinful actions.[3] The desire itself might well be neutral, or even good. The desire for food for example, is a necessary part of human existence, and an occasion for feasting and fellowship, but its distortions can be seen in both greed, that refuses to consider the other, and eating disorders that can blind the sufferer to their true worth. Food, or sex, or possessions, or any of the things that can be the object of our inordinate desires are not in themselves sinful; it is the way in which we use those desires, and especially when we attempt to use them to fill the place that only God can fill, or seek to find our validation and our security in things created rather than the Creator, that they become sinful. When it comes to relationships, if our relationship is built on a need to have our needs met then the other person can become merely an object of desire and not a unique person in their own right.

Unfortunately, Cassian's teaching on the eight different passions, or thoughts (gluttony, lust, avarice, anger, dejection, acedia, vainglory

---

[3] See for example Sr Margaret Mary Funk OSB's exposition of this in *Thoughts Matter: Discovering the Spiritual Journey.* (Collegeville MN: Liturgical Press, 1998). See also the *Conferences* of John Cassian (see p. 20 note 13).

and pride) became, in later teaching by Gregory the Great, the Seven Deadly Sins. Rather than a concentration on thoughts that affect our actions and could be recognised and redirected, the emphasis changed to that of sins to be avoided:

> The emphasis on sin, which this change in terminology both affected and effected, tended to distort the earlier emphasis on training the thoughts for the benefits of a serious seeker who, by striving towards purity of heart, longs intensely for a significant relationship with God.[4]

For Cassian, self-knowledge and awareness of thoughts led to spiritual growth. Here we see how living the Vow of Chastity becomes a serious element in our spiritual growth. Rather than repressing our desires we redirect them into right relationships, primarily with God, but then, through that relationship, with His world. This is not to deny the fact of our ability to sin, but the witness of Scripture is that we are loved despite our failings: 'But God proves His love for us in that while we still were sinners Christ died for us.' (Rom. 5:8).

The experience of faith in God leads us to realise that we do not need to earn love or to be good enough before we can receive love; instead we find ourselves responding in love out of gratitude, a love that claims nothing for itself because it knows itself loved. Cassian in his teaching encourages us to distinguish between life lived in the Spirit and life lived according to the flesh (cf. Rom. 8:5–6). We realise that we do not need the things that we thought we needed to bolster our sense of self-worth, nor do we need to use others to meet our needs. Our identity is found in God, and our relationship to His world is that of grateful stewards and co-creators.

This is an area where many of us struggle. It is often so difficult to love impartially; we need and crave security, satisfaction and affirmation, and we look to our human loves to meet these needs. At its worst, the other becomes simply an object, there to meet my needs,

---

[4] Mary Margaret Funk OSB, *Thoughts Matter: Discovering the Spiritual Journey* (Collegeville MN: Liturgical Press, 1998), 10.

rather than someone with value, their own needs and worth in themselves. To love simply and solely because the other is worthy of love is difficult for us to do. It can be even more difficult when we are faced with the flaws and imperfections of others and know we need to remain in a loving relationship with them. One of the challenges of community living is the realisation that none of us is perfect. We observe the faults of others and become aware of our own faults and failings, and yet remain in relationships. The good news is that God knows our limitations in loving and works with them. We are limited because we are human and because we are influenced by our past history and circumstances.

When an individual takes a Vow of Chastity, he or she embarks on a journey that will result, if they are open to it, in freedom to love the other wholeheartedly and without conditions. This requires both an inner freedom with a healthy sense of self-worth and boundaries, and a deep relationship with God, the source of love. As St Ælred says,

> … as His divine fire grows warmer little by little,
> it wondrously absorbs the other loves into its fullness,
> like so many sparks.[5]

When our loves flow from our love of God, an integration can begin to happen that enables us to love from a heart set on God; the love with which we love others is God's love, flowing through us.

This brings us back to the two aspects of Chastity; the outer practice of celibacy or continence and the inner practice of *the whole being set on God*. Both are important, but the outer practice requires the inner practice in order to bear fruit. The issues that will be faced as a person lives out their vows will vary over the years. In the early days of a vocation, and maybe for some time, this may include mourning the loss of opportunities for relationships and perhaps children. This very real loss must not be repressed but can be an

---

[5] Ælred of Rievaulx, *The Mirror of Charity*, III:2, 3 and 4 in Elizabeth Connor, trans., *Aelred of Rievaulx, Mirror of Charity*, Cistercian Fathers Series, 17 (Kalamazoo MI: Cistercian Publications, 1990).

opportunity for a positive reaffirmation of the path chosen in light of the positive nature of both options. After all, any serious commitment to one path requires a renunciation of other, equally positive possibilities. Care needs to be taken to avoid virtual or substitute relationships to fill what can be experienced as a void. The primary relationship is with God.

The outward practice of celibacy finds expression in many ways; someone may be celibate as a lifestyle choice (whether that is vowed or not); they may be celibate for a particular season or a particular reason (cf. 1 Cor. 7:5), or they may practice continence: sexual relations only within a committed relationship with their partner. This lifestyle choice may or may not have a religious background and may vary at different times in the life of an individual.

Being celibate is in itself no better or worse, and certainly not morally superior, to the vocation of marriage and childbearing. Marriage vows and religious vows both involve a lifestyle that makes conscious decisions regarding an individual's relationship with others. But while marriage draws two people together, the Vow of Chastity sets someone apart in a way that enables a concentration on the love of God, and through God of the world. Both marriage vows and religious vows should lead to a deeper and more authentic compassion for others. Writing about her reflections on the vows in preparation for Profession, Sr Andrea Koverman of the Sisters of Charity wrote:

> Celibacy is not simply the obvious sacrifices: no husband, no sex, no children. Celibacy is the natural and logical result of a passionate quest for God who never fails to intrigue me, to hold my attention and fascinate me. God has a primary claim on me, and what I choose to commit my time and life-energy to. Celibacy is not about living without intimacy, but loving the way that God loves: openly, inclusively, but without exclusive possessiveness. It is not about turning my feelings off but making myself available to an increasingly wider circle of people.[6]

---

[6] http://futureofcharity.blogspot.com/2015/02/it-must-be-love.html (accessed 17 March 2021).

In practice living the Vow of Chastity, or living by a marriage vow, is a lifetime process involving growth in maturity on all levels of our being, including into sexual maturity. Celibacy does not mean repression or prudishness and needs to include a healthy respect and understanding of our body and its needs. Included is a developing sense of healthy boundaries in relationships alongside a growing ability to love impartially. In this way the vow opens up the individual to a freedom to love others in a way that might not be possible in other circumstances.

This emphasis on love of God at the heart of the vow is vital: without it, chastity would be a loveless thing; with it, it is a source of deep hearted compassion for the other. As the *SLG Way of Life* expresses it:

> The practice of chastity should lead us to purity of heart and singleness of purpose; and it is in chastity, which is the whole being set on God, that the hidden joy which is beyond all natural attainment will be found.[7]

Intimate and bridal imagery is used both in Scripture and by many mystical writers, where God is seen as the bridegroom and the individual soul as the bride. In *The Spiritual Canticle* St John of the Cross tells of the journey of the individual soul into God in the form of a love story using this imagery:

> There you will show me
> That which my soul desired;
> And there You will give at once,
> O You, my life!
> That which You gave me the other day.[8]

This is not an attempt to replace a forbidden physical relationship with a spiritual imagined alternative. Rather it is a recognition that all our relationships, at their best, are modelled on that perfect relationship within the Trinity.

---

[7] 'Chastity' in *SLG Way of Life*, 20.
[8] St John of the Cross, *Spiritual Canticle*, verse xxxviii.

The prophet Hosea uses similar imagery:

> Therefore, I will now allure her,
>   and bring her into the wilderness,
>   and speak tenderly to her.
>
> (Hos. 2:14).

The Song of Songs, sometimes dismissed in modern times as 'merely an erotic love song', was understood by the Fathers of the Church as a metaphor for the journey of the soul into God.

> Set me as a seal upon your heart,
>   as a seal upon your arm;
> for love is strong as death,
>   passion fierce as the grave.
> Its flashes are flashes of fire,
>   a raging flame.
> Many waters cannot quench love,
>   neither can floods drown it.
>
> (Song of Songs 8:6–7)

This is a fierce and deep love; if intimate love as an image is such a potent sign of the relationship with God, then all our other loves have the potential to mirror that relationship. As St Ælred suggests, growth in chastity, when lived as a way towards a deeper love of God, 'wondrously absorbs the other loves into its fulness'.

In the Bible the concept of purity has the suggestion of something unalloyed, unmixed. As individuals we so often find that our thoughts and our hearts are distracted and overtaken by myriad concerns, anxieties and worries. Many things compete for our allegiance and we are often unsure where to find our security. In the Sermon on the Mount, Jesus promises us: 'Blessed are the pure in heart, for they will see God.' (Matt. 5:8).

The Vow of Chastity aims to lead us towards that purity of heart, not by preventing us from engaging in something that is seen as sinful, but by enabling us to love more purely and wholeheartedly with a love that has its source in God and not in our own need.

St Ælred describes three loves: love of God, love of neighbour, and love of self. When our love of self and of others flows from our love of God then all three are brought to perfection. Here, as the *SLG Rule* says, is that 'hidden joy which is beyond all natural attainment'. Chastity is one way to this goal and, for the monastic, a road to a deeper love of God and of the world.

—◆—

THE VOW OF OBEDIENCE
Sr Judith SLG

Life is full of choices, and so, full of obedience. Obedience is something we *all* do whether we are aware of it or not. Advertising plays on obedience, that is how it works; it influences what we will be obedient to and which choice we will make. It occurs to me to speculate what Christian advertising might look like. Perhaps the nearest we have had in recent times (in the UK during the COVID-19 pandemic) were the government slogans of 'Stay home. Protect the NHS. Save lives.' This is a message influencing our choice; our obedience to it has a benefit to society and like all choices it involves a loss, in some ways it cuts off options. We can choose not to be obedient to it, and both obedience and disobedience have consequences.

Those of us who have made a Vow of Obedience have only made visible and explicit our intention and desire to be obedient life-long to very specific things: God and the Gospel, mediated through the community in which we live. The act of making the vow publicly and in the context of the Church provides us with support and enables our freedom to go on making this choice again and again. In the ceremony in which we make our vows the first question the person making the vow is asked is 'What do you desire?' and their answer is 'The Mercy of God and the liberty to bind myself to Him'. That liberty is a crucial hint about what the vows are about and what they are for. Like the government's slogan bringing freedom from disease, the vows bring us an inner freedom, though both entail things that, at a superficial glance, can look like the opposite of freedom. Jane Williams summarizes it well in her book *Perfect Freedom*:

> There is no such thing as freedom. We are all constrained by something. The aim, then, is to choose what you will be obedient to, and to allow that obedience to free you more and more from other kinds of slavery.[1]

---

[1] Jane Williams, *Perfect Freedom: Becoming the Person We Were Meant to Be*, Borders Series (Norwich: Canterbury Press, 2001), 2.

It is a bit like pruning a tree; the choice and its limitations channel the life force in the chosen direction. It ensures that all the energy and life force of the tree goes in the right direction and so too, we hope, with the vows.

The word obedience has its roots in the Latin *audire* meaning to listen or to hear, to do what you have heard. This gives a strong indication of the connection to choice. What 'voice' are we going to listen to? How do we pay attention to what we hear? Even that obedience may have something to do with what we choose to listen or expose ourselves to. We are listening to things all the time, we decide which voices we will give importance and which we will ignore. Rowan Williams describes this well in his sermon on St Oswald of Worcester (*d.* 992) where he is describing St Oswald's habit of washing the feet of the poor, something he did even on the last day of his life.

> Obeying is having our ears open, in readiness to hear how the commands of God are uttered to us in the facts of suffering. It isn't that God crisply passes on instructions, so that we know just what the right thing is to do: *how* we respond requires thought and care, patience and—sometimes—depressingly hard and compromising labour. But obedience begins in responding to a primary summons to *look* and *listen*: not to lie to ourselves about the kind of world this is.[2]

A Vow of Obedience hones our listening, exposes us to our inner voices and trains us, hopefully, to spot the subtle influences on our lives more easily. Obviously in a monastic context we are wanting to be obedient to God and the Gospel; wanting to hear those voices more strongly and easily than any other. Experience tends to show that our own will can 'muffle' our ears, so to speak, blow us off course or even downright mislead us. This is where being in a community where there are others around who can act as checks and balances comes in handy. It must also be said that being in a position where you have the authority to ask for obedience means you need

[2] Rowan Williams, *A Ray of Darkness: Sermons and Reflections* (Oxford: Cowley Publications, 1995), 172.

to be able to listen very closely yourself and be able to tell the difference between power and authority. It is when the difference between the two is not fully understood that abuse can occur.

What the *SLG Rule* says of obedience is that it is, 'the means by which the human will is re-established in its true purpose to be one with the will of God'. I tend to think of that in terms of a stringed instrument with sympathetic strings, like the Sitar. When the main string is plucked the sympathetic string, if it is properly in tune with the main string, will vibrate of its own accord ('in sympathy'), giving off its own sound and adding an extra quality to the overall tone. Our wills, if they are 'in tune' will vibrate with the will of God and add a dimension to the 'sound'. Living out the vow acts like tuning the string.

Our ordinary daily lives together in community require us to be obedient to God, to attend and listen to Him, each other and circumstances. Patient silence makes 'voices' — that may be coming from our depths, our past, our instinct, our conditioning — more audible, and allows us to sift them and choose whether to listen to them or not. It is in this gentle attention that gradually we come to hear the voice that calls us to our freedom to be the human being God created us uniquely to be, in relation to God, each other and our universe.

In practice this means there are many 'tools', simple things to which we are obedient: the timetable of the monastic day and Liturgical Hours and year, the practicalities of living together, the needs of the individuals around us and the group as a whole, the needs of the Church and of the world. Perhaps I can give a personal example: I am not someone who wakes up easily or is generally at my best before 10 a.m. in the morning, but the monastic timetable asks of me that I rise at 5.30 a.m. I can testify that after thirty years this is not any easier! Yet obedience means that I drag myself out of bed most mornings because doing so enables me to have silent time to create space to listen at the precious beginning of the day; it enables me to share worship with my sisters and pray and praise for the world. It teaches me that while my duvet feels like heaven on earth at that hour, my desire *is* to live a life of prayer in fellowship with my sisters, so to listen to the voice that says 'turn over and go back to sleep' when the alarm goes off is not actually the voice of freedom or my deepest desire. While this can be difficult to remember at that hour of the morning, actually my true freedom lies in doing what is mundanely asked of me, to get up, and then gradually I can reconnect with tuning in to the voice of my deepest desire, which is to tune into the voice of God within. The Liturgical Hour of prayer and praise is a two-way street: yes, I try to be obedient to being there and to saying the words with attention and love, thus offering my prayer and praise to God, but as a Desert Father story goes, it works on me too.

> Abba John ... asked Abba Poemen about the problem that our heart is so hard ... The old man said 'The nature of water is soft, that of stone is hard; but if a bottle is hung above the stone, allowing the water to fall drop by drop, it wears away the stone. So it is with the word of God; it is soft and our heart is hard, but the man who hears the word of God often, opens his heart to the fear of God.[3]

Thus obedience to the act of getting out of bed and turning up in chapel is part of my re-creation, part of setting me free to be the human being God created me to be.

Being attentive or obedient to the practicalities of life together in community provides small and large occasions to practice obedience; the 'dailyness' of life together means some, like the tiny choice of finishing up leftovers at supper, are repeated almost constantly. But even the little things can have a deeper significance: by not being able to choose what I eat and when (one of the constraints of being in community) I can stand in solidarity with all those who have no choice through poverty or being in prison. I can make it an act of prayer for, say, the Uighur people in China. It also works on me, showing me where I am not yet truly free; where I am still hemmed in by my preferences. It still amazes me how difficult I can find it, how much resistance and how many excuses my mind and will can come up with.

---

[3] Abba Poemen saying 183, translated from the French collection of Dom Lucien Regnault, *Sentences des Pères du Désert Collection Alphabetique* (Sablé-sur-Sarthe: Abbaye Saint-Pierre de Solesmes, 1981), 260 (para. 757).

If my 'will is to be re-established in its true purpose to be one with the will of God'[4] then surely something as small as this ought to be simple?! But my experience is that it is not, and the dailyness of the encounters with that gradually begin to alert me to the fact and help to re-train my will, so that when more costly choices come along I am better prepared.

When obedience comes in the form of doing something I have been asked to do that I do not want to do, it can be both difficult and costly, but again will reveal, perhaps, where I am still not truly free from my own self-will and so give me the chance to be 'more and more free' from *that* kind of 'slavery', as Jane Williams writes. Sometimes it will also offer its own unexpected gift. I think of being told that I needed to recuperate from a major operation away from the convent. At the time, feeling physically weak and rather vulnerable, all I wanted was to be in my familiar surroundings where I could 'dip into' the worshipping life of the community when I was able to; the last thing I wanted was a long coach journey home. In obedience to those who wanted me to recuperate away from the convent I went home. My recovery was not straightforward, and rather than a couple of weeks I was away for five weeks which included Holy Week, Easter and my birthday. A couple of years later my mother was diagnosed with a life threatening illness and died eighteen months later. Those five weeks of just 'being' with her enabled me to approach her passing with a sense of completion, of my having had time with her and she with me. It went some way towards healing the hurt that often arises in families when someone chooses to enter a convent. For my birthday she asked what I would like and gave me a copy of *Celebrating Daily Prayer* which I was using at the time as a shortened form of Office.[5] She wrote in the front of it and I use it each time I go away, a permanent reminder of that precious time, and of her. Although at the time I was much the worse for wear from the journey and angry at the imposition of

---

[4] 'Obedience' in *SLG Rule*, ch. 11.

[5] David Stancliffe (Bishop of Salisbury), *Celebrating Daily Prayer* (London: Bloomsbury Academic, Pocket edition 2003).

it, today I can recognise the temporary nature of the sickness and appreciate the deeper gift that was given in that time.

This illustrates where something was against my will: a conflict between what I believed was in my own best interests and what the person asking me to recuperate away believed was in my own best interests. What cannot legitimately be asked by obedience is for someone to go against a prayerfully and carefully-discerned matter of conscience, and our Rule protects that. Obviously I could not say that going home was a matter of conscience, which would have been to abuse the protection in the Rule, but it seems important while talking about going against one's will that the distinction between will and conscience is clear.

Listening to circumstances can mean being obedient to the needs of the planet, really exposing myself to uncomfortable facts and choices. I may not be in a position to choose to avoid plastic packaging but I can be obedient to the need to use less energy, not to have my radiator on with the window open or to take the time to cut up my non-recyclable plastic and capture it in an eco-brick. These simple prosaic actions are one facet of the listening that obedience requires of us. Psalm 119, that song of the joy of walking in God's commandments and Law, says in v. 45 'I will walk at liberty because I study your commandments'. 'The Law' covers many detailed observances that are there to be obeyed because they enable people to walk rightly with God and neighbour, and therefore give the person a true liberty: freedom from causing harm to self or others. Obedience to the needs of the planet can therefore quite easily be seen as commensurate with the liberty the psalm talks about and the whole of the Law seeks to create. It is also an acknowledgement and reminder of the fact that I am a creature, created by God, for God. Taking care of creation is an act of honouring God. So, although cutting up that plastic can seem to be a time-consuming irritation, if I do it remembering God's creation and my place in it, it can set me in right relationship with both my creator and my fellow creatures. That way it becomes reverence for both God and the whales and again frees me to be the human being I am, with my unique and responsible place in God's scheme of things.

Our model of obedience is Christ himself. It can be tempting to think that He was God incarnate and therefore obedience was a simple act of being in tune with the will of the Father. But if we look more closely at the Gospel we can see instances where it would appear it was not straightforward for Him either. Take the episode with the Syrophoenician woman (Mark 7:24–30). Christ is clear that His mission is 'to the lost sheep of the house of Israel' (Matt. 15:24) yet the woman's remarkable persistence and answers to Him result in Him 'hearing' His Father's will anew. John V. Taylor describes this process vividly in his sermon 'The True Kingdom' which is worth reading in full. I quote only the climax below

> ... then why did He turn to them with the words, "I have been sent only to the lost sheep of the house of Israel" unless they were spoken out of an inward struggle and perplexity? Then, as we do if we are wise, He put his problem squarely to the one who had raised it "It is not right to take the children's food and throw it to the dogs." There in its full harshness is the doctrine of exclusiveness, and Jesus stated it blatantly as though challenging her to help Him: "So, what am I to do?" Back comes her answer: "Yes, but even the dogs live on the scraps that fall from their master's table."
>
> O woman, daughter of Tyre, with your cheeky courage, great is your faith, for it launched the universal, world-wide, catholic Church! Let us never forget that you and I and virtually the whole of Christendom are the dogs. The knowledge of Christ is available to us only because of Jesus's commitment to inclusiveness, only because of his response to that moment of revelation when the God of the scriptures appeared to change His mind.[6]

In the garden of Gethsemane too we see Jesus listening, struggling with His own will and His understanding of what the Father's will might be. "My Father, if it is possible, let this cup pass from me. Yet not what I want, but what you want." (Matt. 26:39). The Letter to the Philippians tells us that Christ 'became obedient to the point of death — even death on a Cross' (Phil. 2:8). And Hebrews 5:8 tells us that

---

[6] John V. Taylor, 'The True Kingdom', in *The Easter God and His Easter People* (London: Continuum, 2003), 97.

'Although He was a son, He learned obedience through what He suffered'. He *learned* obedience. I understand that to mean that it did not come ready-formed but was something that grew in him, from the time He learned obedience to Mary and Joseph in Nazareth, to learning obedience to the Law, to learning obedience in His mission and right up to the end of life, to death—and an agonizing, humiliating death. In all these circumstances Jesus listened and sought, through that listening, to discern and act according to the will of the Father. So we could paraphrase the Philippians verse as 'Christ carried on listening for the will of the Father and did it even up to death, even listening through the death of crucifixion.' That is our model of obedience: constantly listening all though our lives, even to its last moment, even through agony.

I have sometimes heard preaching that leans towards using the verse from Philippians to imply that Jesus went so far in His obedience as to be willing to die, to go through death, with the obvious or even explicitly stated question 'are *you* willing to do whatever God asks even if it means death?', but my experience of living a Vow of Obedience has led me to think this is not the way to hear that verse. It is not that Jesus went *that* far, but more simply, that Jesus just went on listening, and the amazing thing is that He still managed to listen even through the agony of crucifixion. Certainly my own experience of trying to listen is that it can get harder when I am pushed to extremes of any sort, physical pain, tiredness or sadness.

Each Holy Cross Day (14 September) Carmelites renew their vows. On that day in 1939 Sr Teresa Benedicta of the Cross (Edith Stein) who was a Carmel in Echt in the Netherlands wrote an exhortation for the Renewal of Vows that included the following:

> Through the faithful observance of the Vows you make your heart free and open; and then the floods of that divine love will be able to flow into it, making it overflow and bear fruit to the furthest reaches of the earth.[7]

---

[7] From the Propers for the Feast of St Teresa Benedicta of the Cross (Edith Stein), 9 August: *Discalced Carmelite Proper Offices of Carmelite Saints and Blesseds in the Liturgy of the Hours* (Scotts Valley CA: CreateSpace Independent Publishing Platform, 2017), 129.

The faithful observance of her vows for seven short years (1935–42) formed in her the freedom she wrote about, and meant that those who survived their transportation to Auschwitz with her could testify to her comforting those around her even as she walked to the gas chambers. She is an example of the liberty the Vow of Obedience can create. Like St Oswald, listening to God in the facts of the neighbour suffering next to her, and to the circumstances right until the end of her life like her Lord and Saviour. As the Collect for Feasts of Mary in *Common Worship* calls it: 'the joyful path of obedience'.

—◆—

CONTEMPLATION AND ENCLOSURE
Sr Eileen Mary SLG

How can we shake off the dead weight of images and misconceptions that have encrusted themselves around the words *contemplation* and *enclosure*; how convey the spirit of adventure and seeking and finding that draws the contemplative on without the carrot of outward success or visible results?

For many outside the monastic life the impression of a convent or monastery is often either informed by fictional or biographical movies depicting the lives of monks or nuns that show nothing of the practical changes engendered by life in the twenty-first century, or by the romanticised image of Gerard Manley Hopkins' beautiful poem 'Heaven-Haven', subtitled 'A nun takes the veil'. To the secular, *Enclosure* can suggest an element of imprisonment; this for some is alarming and may be the main reason they hold back from considering the monastic life. However, particularly in the modern world, nothing could be further from reality: the enclosure is a sacred space in which the monastic calling is exemplified; it is what defines monastic life as opposed to secular living. All religious communities, even those dedicated to the care of the sick or to teaching, have some element of it, some part of their physical living space from which those outside the sacramental life are excluded.

In the early days of monastic life many of the domestic tasks necessary to life were undertaken by novices or lay brothers and sisters, but nowadays with our communities smaller and with fewer young members many of those activities fall to secular employees, so the enclosure is no longer quite as strictly observed in many communities as it once was. Nevertheless, for communities of nuns, secular staff admitted to the enclosure are usually only women, and in communities of monks, only men.

For three and a half centuries, until the Second Vatican Council, countless convents both in Europe and in Central and South America were erected in strict accordance with injunctions set down first by

St Charles Borromeo in 1572 and elaborated in 1599.[1] His description of a convent indeed sounds more like a prison than a sacred enclosure to us: not only the height of walls but the precise construction of the one door to the outside world, and even the types of vegetation that might be planted against the walls are set out in painstaking detail. This document has understandably been largely responsible for the somewhat negative attitude towards enclosure today. I would doubt whether Borromeo would have considered these lines from T. S. Eliot in his poem 'The Dry Salvages' at all relevant to the contemplative life:

> Here and there does not matter
> We must be still and still moving
> Into another intensity
> For a further union, a deeper communion.

Rather than focussing on the exclusion of the outside world therefore, enclosure or withdrawal today is considered as a Christian discipline to support a contemplation that is open to all. Different vocations will demand different forms of enclosure within this wide definition, but the fact itself finds its inspiration in the primary doctrines of the Christian faith:

The enclosure of the incarnation—the limitless, immeasurable Divine Life enclosed in time, space and matter. As far as we know, Jesus lived for most of His life in one small village among one group of people. All that He spilled out later in acts and words in His ministry had been learned in that long probation and quiet pondering on what the relationship between God, humanity and creation really meant. He had considered the lilies, watched the woman

---

[1] St Charles Borromeo, Archbishop of Milan 1564–84, prepared the *Injunctions for Religious Women* for the Archdiocese of Milan in 1572. This was formalized in the *Acta Ecclesiae Mediolanensis*, the legal acts of the Milanese Church, first published in 1582 to disseminate the legislation sponsored by St Charles Borromeo. The legislation is widely viewed as the consequence of the Council of Trent (1565). The last publication of the *Acta Ecclesiae Mediolanensis* was curated by Achille Ratti (later Pope Pius XI) in the last decade of the nineteenth century.

sweeping to find her silver coin and the sower sowing his seed, and had learned to see through the most ordinary things, their eternal dimensions and meaning.

The enclosure of redemption—the passing of that life through the eye of the needle of death, the utmost limitation of the Cross opening up to the life of Resurrection that *is* the life of contemplation.

The enclosure of unity—when all were assembled together with one mind in one place and the Holy Spirit was given to transform the infant Church into a eucharistic unity.

The contemplative tries to live within these enclosures and in relation to them, not for their own sake but because they believe that a life lived out under these conditions is the surest way of bringing the Resurrection of Christ and His kingdom into the world of the here and now.

Therefore we think first of all of enclosure as a Christian principle and discipline, not confined to those who have accepted it voluntarily as a life-long obligation but as something that at some time and in some measure may be experienced by anyone who has gone beyond a merely nominal Christianity; those who through sickness, imprisonment, relationships or work have been nailed to a situation in which there has been no possibility of manipulation, and who have been forced in it to face the element of restraint, limitation, stability — in conflict or boredom—that is the essence of enclosure.

Contemplation in this context does not mean contemplative prayer as such, but a quality of life that is contemplative: one that is lived vertically in relationship to God rather than horizontally in relationship to time and those around us. In which those primary mysteries of incarnation, redemption and unity are lived out within and through the disciplines of a standing place that has been accepted in faith and love and used creatively. As Thomas Merton pointed out in an article called 'Openness and Cloister', this relationship between contemplation and enclosure is one of agape: surrender to the inexplicable mercy that comes to us from God entirely on His own terms, in the context of our personal and social history, rather than the yearning of the human heart for the vision of beauty.[2] Merton does not exclude eros, that force which started us all off on our Christian and religious way, but always it has to be placed in a secondary position. Elsewhere he explains:

> Today a new and more biblical understanding of the contemplative life is called for: we must see it as a response to the dynamic Word of God in history, we must see it in the light of biblical eschatology. The contemplative finds God not in the embrace of 'pure love' alone, but in the prophetic ardour of response to the 'word of God'. Not in love experienced as essential good, but in love that breaks through into the world of sinful men in the fire of judgement and mercy. The contemplative must see love not only as the highest and purest experience of the human heart transformed by grace, but as God's unfailing fidelity to unfaithful man.[3]

For *eros* is the hunger for divine love that we possess, not because we are holy, but because we are human. Like all human hungers it will be satisfied, but in God's own time and in His own way, not through discontent with our own vocation and through surrender to the temptation to think that we will do better in different and more propitious circumstances.

God's agape can break through into all circumstances as the story of His people repeatedly shows. Deuteronomy recalls Israel's enclosure in the wilderness and God's action upon them there:

> Remember the long way that the Lord your God has led you these forty years in the wilderness, in order to humble you, testing you to know what was in your heart, whether or not you would keep His commandments. He humbled you by letting you hunger, then by feeding you with manna, with which neither you nor your ancestors were acquainted, in order to make you understand that one does not live by bread alone, but by every word that comes from the mouth of the Lord.   (Deut. 8:2–3)

---

[2] Thomas Merton, 'Openness and Cloister', *Cistercian Studies Quarterly* 2/4 (1967), 312–23.

[3] Thomas Merton, *Contemplation in a World of Action* (London: Allen & Unwin, 1971), 133.

As Merton says, humanity's agape consists of the prophetic ardour in which we respond to this Word of God that comes to us through vocation and its demands. He continues:

> God speaks to us not only in the Bible, not only in the secret inspirations of our own hearts, but also through the public and manifest events of our own time and above all through the Church ... In the light of the Council it is no longer possible even for contemplatives to simply shut out the world, to ignore it, to forget it, in order to relish the private joys of contemplative eros. To insist on the cultivation of total recollection for the sake of this eros and its consolations would be pure and simple selfishness. It would also mean a failure really to deepen the true Christian dimensions of agape which are the real dimensions of the contemplative life. This is where so much confusion arises.[4]

So the enclosed garden of peace and joy of our dreams, where the distortions and disturbances of life and human nature never come and where we shall enjoy God alone, is largely an illusion and certainly not the essence of the contemplative and enclosed life. Monica Furlong is nearer the mark when she says:

> The Christian life can all be done on the spot. On this square foot of ground on which we stand we experience crucifixion and resurrection (if we are not so taken up with manipulating life that nothing can happen to us) and this is action, the action of love. Only the moment matters. That is where God is.[5]

The essential pressure of enclosures lie not in the physical conditions but from the fact that we are enclosed in time as well as in space. There is room for manoeuvre and compensation in the environments in which those in unenclosed situations live their lives: a different face is presented at work from that which is shown in the family circle or in our social lives; a failure in one situation may be compensated for by success in another. It is only too easy to avoid meeting the person that we really are when we are consumed by the changing

---

[4] Merton, 'Openness and Cloister'.
[5] Monica Furlong, *Travelling In* (London: Hodder and Stoughton, 1971), 98.

expressions of personality in different aspects of our daily lives. We can be so busy wearing these different personalities though, that we avoid meeting the person that we are before God, with a potential and vocation known to Him alone. Yet in the kingdom of God it is only *this* person who has any reality.

In the enclosure we are faced with the inescapable fact of being the same person all the time, among the same people and in circumstances that do not vary appreciably. This is possible only if we are prepared to face the cost of reality: there are certainly personalities for whom this type of life is incredibly stressful, since it requires change from the person the outside world has shaped us to be, and sometimes our mental makeup is simply not designed for this sort of life. Entering an enclosure inevitably becomes a situation of judgement, not only on the individual, but on the historical and sociological chain of cause and effect that has made us what we are, and that will continue to condition us as long as we live only along the line of time. The new life engendered by enclosure breaks through when we accept a total solidarity with both our past and our environment, not using what was wrong in them to excuse ourselves, but exposing both good and bad to the judgement and mercy of God.

The humility of dependence on something or someone greater than the self is the only way the treadmill of cause and effect can be halted and a new thing allowed to enter into the world. To live in the power of this undeserved, inexplicable mercy of God is *contemplative life*, something that keeps a person anchored in their right place in relation to God, neighbours and self. Many people who would consider themselves 'quite ordinary' come through this testing purified by it if they have within them the seed of agape, even if they do not explicitly recognise the life as that of the crucified and risen Christ at the heart of the experience.

> Enter through the narrow gate; for the gate is wide and the road is easy that leads to destruction, and there are many who take it. For the gate is narrow and the road is hard that leads to life, and there are few who find it. (Matt. 7:13–14)

Again I tell you, it is easier for a camel to go through the eye of a needle than for someone who is rich to enter the kingdom of God.

(Matt. 19:24)

This Gospel paradox is not an injunction to obey the Law of Moses to the letter, but an invitation to go through the gates, narrow as a needle's eye, discarding all the baggage that would make it impossible to pass through, and so enter into the new quality of life that is offered to us. However, all this could be distorted into a cult of suffering were it not for the enclosure of incarnation that is the bedrock on which it rests.

In the full Christian doctrine of incarnation, the expectation is that the fruits of redemption should make a person not less, but more human, and thus each person should find themselves in a relationship to creation of priest and servant. This is spoken of in Romans 8: 'For the creation waits with eager longing for the revealing of the children of God.' (Rom. 8:19).

The Fathers of the fourth century did not go out into the Egyptian desert in order to transcend the material but to liberate the spirit, so that the body could become its supple natural instrument. So, although according to present-day standards their types of ascetic practice were exaggerated and sometimes competitive, yet an account of St Antony, emerging from his cave after twenty years is relevant to a modern experience of enclosure:

When they saw him they marvelled to see that his body kept his former state, being neither grown heavy for want of exercise nor shrunken with fastings and strivings against demons. For he was such as they had known him before his retirement. The light of his soul too was absolutely pure. It was not shrunken with grieving nor dissipated by pleasure; it had no touch of levity nor of gloom. He was not bashful at seeing the crowd nor elated at being welcomed by such large numbers but was unvaryingly tranquil, a man ruled by reason, whose whole character had grown firm-set in the way that nature had meant it to grow.[6]

---

[6] St Athanasius, *Life of St Antony*, trans. Dom J. B. Mclaughlin OSB (New York: Burns, Oates and Washbourne, 1924), 22.

The enclosure of the desert was functional, not a mystique. No walls shut out the world. The enclosure was a disciplined choice, a special type of seeking for God.

To know the full dimensions of contemplative agape, the discipline of enclosure has to be balanced by that of openness. Throughout the history of the church there have been saints who have maintained this tradition. Counter-Reformation thought about enclosure was dependent upon concepts of divine transcendence and eternity that were as much Platonic as Christian in origin. The actual stuff of human life was regarded negatively and as matter for distraction, so the attempt was made to resolve the dichotomy between sacred and secular by eliminating the secular as far as possible.

Today it is the secular itself that frequently constitutes the environment of the desert. Multi-storey flats rise out of a labyrinth of streets and houses, and here there is much of the loneliness and sense of de-personalisation that was experienced by the hermit in the course of his penitential isolation. God is giving to many nowadays the vocation to be contemplatives in the world, in order to teach us how to use this experience creatively. It is as Christ is brought, through prayer and love, to occupy this modern enclosure that others will feel the attractiveness of His presence and come with their needs to knock at the door. Always the outgoingness has to be matched with the withdrawal; yet for the openness to be effective the proportion of withdrawal needs to be far greater than is usually recognised.

Achieving unity is a struggle, since the enclosure unfailingly brings to the surface those human passions, desires and fears that are responsible for most of the troubles of humanity. The occasions of conflict may seem small compared with those of the world's disorders, yet the passions aroused are of the same nature, and the contemplative believes that through their penitence and return to God, spiritual healing is thereby released into the world. We are all of one flesh in Adam and in Christ, otherwise our belief in such a communication—which is neither physical nor psychic, but spiritual—would be meaningless, and our service to the Church a delusion.

I have deliberately fluctuated between contemplation and enclosure as lived in the monastic enclosed life and the element of enclosure that should be present in every Christian life. I believe profoundly in particular vocations, each being called to live out some single aspect of the total infinite Christ for the family of the Church as a whole. Yet no vocation can stand on its own. If it is authentically Christian the same elements for which it stands must appear in varying intensity and conditions in the life of all Christians who may be helped by those who have tested its implications and demands to the fullest possible extent.

So we return again to the proposition that enclosure is an element of the essence of Christianity that supports and disciplines a contemplation open to all, but that the types and intensities of enclosure will vary tremendously according to the vocation it supports.

The spirit of Carmel, that has had a vital influence on the ethos of the Sisters of the Love of God has always contained within itself the possibility of a limited apostolate towards those who wish to learn something of the inner life. This is borne out in an essay written by Thomas Merton in his book *Disputed Questions*, which gives a valuable account of the history and spirit of the Carmelite Order. He writes:

> The Carmelite apostolate has, ideally speaking, this very special modality of its own. It is a contemplative apostolate to other potential contemplatives. It is an apostolate of interior prayer. ... what it teaches above all is the way of the hidden life. And here above all, *nemo dat quod non habet,* no one can give something which he does not himself have.[7]

This conception of enclosure in relation to contemplation and openness is not necessarily that of other traditions, and discovering the true tradition of each community is about understanding both its essence and the effects of being grounded in a certain period of history.

---

[7] Thomas Merton, *Disputed Questions* (New York: Farrar, Straus and Giroux, 1960), part III, 'Light in Darkness: The Ascetic Doctrine of St John of the Cross', section 1.

If we are clear about the principles on which we stand, there can be great flexibility, both in the working out of the community vocation as a whole and in the lives of individual members. If the vision expressed in the Rule and teaching of the community is wide and deep enough, any individual expression of it will relate closely to the eucharistic body of which it is a part, and that must be kept together as a living, working entity through mutual charity and obedience in the vertical dimension in which contemplative life is lived.

———◆———

THE CELL
Sr Isabel SLG

Within the wider space of the monastic enclosure, where secular participants may intrude from time to time, there is one space that remains very much as it always was, the private space that entirely excludes the secular world: the cell.

Within the desert of the early solitaries was the cell, but this was seen and spoken of again and again by the Desert Fathers as the one spot in which, if we stood and allowed things to happen to us without escaping physically or mentally, a change would ultimately take place that would transfigure our whole relationship with God, the self and the world.

We cannot separate the solitary aspect of our life entirely from what is corporate, but the cell is a place, primarily, of solitude. Phrases in the *SLG Rule* and tradition, such as,

… the whole being set on God
… a continual exercise of love and desire reaching out towards God
… chastity of pure intention
… the desire to be set wholly on God

immediately direct us to the vertical thrust of our life Godward, so perhaps it is useful to consider our horizontal relationships as being gathered up into this vertical; the vital part played by the common life in the cleansing and re-direction of desire.

This vertical thrust of our being into which everything that is common to us is to be gathered focusses our attention on the cell, because it is the cell that in a very tangible way epitomizes what is common to us all and, at the same time, what is unique about each of us. The cell is not an invariable feature even of the contemplative orders: some regard their cells simply as a private place to sleep and wash, perhaps to work in, and that is all.

What the *SLG Rule* says about the cell leaves us in no doubt as to its place in our life at that second level of commonness in which we

share a particular vocation within the total vocation of the redeemed
Body of Christ. It says:

> Life and prayer in the cell is an essential element in the Sisters' vo-
> cation. They shall therefore learn to regard their cell as a place
> where the Holy Spirit will reveal to them the Mysteries of God and
> manifest to them the compassion and love of the Saviour.[1]

This solitary dimension in the life of the Sisters of the Love of
God is absolutely built into their vocation, and this has to be grasped
from the outset. Particular developments of this solitary strand (such
as sisters who live as hermits) are secondary to what we are particularly concerned with here. The cell is part of the essence of our
monastic life. If we were to take away life and prayer in the cell as
an essential element we would have something different in our
whole ethos—it would effect a change right through the life—affect-
ing the corporate life as well as the personal, because in our
corporate life we are expressing what in our solitary life we are becoming. If our growth in holiness, in personal relationship with God,
is actually conditional upon the truth of our human relationships
(the love and trust that is built up through our daily encounters on
the horizontal), then we will not go to the cell to get out of the common life, or even to re-charge our batteries for its conflicts and
challenges, but because we are basing our corporate life on our solitude. God forms us in solitude to enable us to express in the common
life what it is to have been face to face with God.

We have to be sure that the person who approaches God in the
solitude of the cell is the same rather unsatisfactory person our
sisters have seen, the disorderly being who cannot altogether be
hidden behind the ordered way of life, or good manners, but will
break out in one way or another. This is the self who approaches
God, this flawed self—not the 'spiritual life' person, not just our
praying, Bible-reading side, but the whole self, just as it has turned
out to be, comes before God in the cell, just as the whole self is in-
flicted upon, or shared with, our sisters.

---

[1] *SLG Rule*, ch. 13.

Even in the cell we are still opening the whole being to God within the common life because it is the common life that actually provides the solitary cell. It is the respect and care of the common life that is acting on our behalf from the very beginning, that gives us what we need in order to follow our heart's desire. Our very coming here amounts to a declaration that we have a naked intent towards God. The common life takes the intention and gives us the means of realising it. The common life provides for the whole of us but it will not run our cell life for us with the same sort of support with which it runs our corporate life for us. Here in the cell we really are alone with our own self. We take into it all that we are, our common humanity, our common baptismal endowment, our unique personhood, and what we are probably most conscious of when we find ourselves alone: our unique individuality. We are entrusted from the start with what we might find a rather overwhelming privacy for as long as we remain in the cell. It is a privacy that is respected from first to last, but it is also a privacy that is both ours and not ours. Nobody will invade it, nobody will relieve our solitude, there are no demands of hospitality on us at all, we never have to entertain anyone in the cell. Even so it is not a privacy that, being so completely ours, we can somehow make cosy and warm by filling it up with things that stamp it with our personal identity and make it our home: the personal items that we feel drawing us irresistibly as soon as we come within the radius of their attraction.

The privacy of our cell is one that paradoxically we share in common with everyone else. Bareness, sameness, is the essence of every cell; it is empty of everything that makes life cosy and companionable, and the challenge or invitation to dance in the pattern of the common life becomes here the invitation to sit still at the heart of the dance. This becomes possible for us only as we become as bare as the cell: if we think of our created life as having a natural point of rest in God, of the movement of the divine love in us tending upward by nature. As a way of looking at the spiritual life, the cell represents in time and space that point of rest in its physical aspect. Although God can encounter us anywhere, at any moment, the cell is the place set apart for personal encounter with God, for the development of that unique between-ness that exists at the most fundamental level and that can begin to pervade our consciousness, even fitfully, only as we give it our attention in solitude.

Accepting the gift of the cell as the appointed meeting place for this thing between God and me, I can think of it in two (of many possible) ways. I can think of the cell as that place that I *enter*, to which my deepest desire tends, that corresponds to that desire, strictness and fundamental bareness. Underneath and through all the tangle of desire on more superficial levels, it is the place where I shall show myself willing to submit to having all my desires re-ordered and re-directed; where my energies, physical and spiritual, will be renewed and refreshed.

On the other hand, I can think of it as the place that, from time to time, I *leave*, in obedience to the invitation or claims of the common life. This attitude to the cell as a place that we leave assumes that the cell is the place where we most habitually and appropriately live. We leave it only in obedience to the common life when the timetable or some special task or need calls us out to be with the others, or to serve them. This means that, but for such calls, the cell is where we would normally be. Therefore when we do leave the cell, it is a good thing to be quite clear why we are doing it, rather than leaving the cell without knowing why each time. In this way we will come to think of going to the cell as going *back* to the cell. If this attitude gets built into our conscious thought, we may find in time that we never actually leave the cell. Because when we are responding to the invitation of the common life, even in the most perfect give-and-take of human relationships that grow out of that life of solitude, we are still a solitary, and this corresponds to our deepest desire and to this essential element, this strand that runs throughout our common life.

There is not much to choose between these two ways of looking at the cell as a means of building up a certain habit of mind, but in either attitude we can see a reflection of the life of the Blessed Trinity, the Word eternally in the bosom of the Father, sent forth by Him to take His part and fulfil His mission in the thick of the world of speech and action. Then, having glorified Him on earth, going back to the Father as the first of many brethren, glorified by His obedience, releasing the power and presence of the Holy Spirit into the world He has redeemed. We could explore that thought infinitely in relation to the cell.

The common life makes this immensely exhilarating and hopeful assumption about each one of us: that we have within us, at least in germ, a unique relationship with God our Creator; the cell will do everything in its power to help us to grow in the common life towards His glory. However, out of respect for the intense privacy of what the cell represents, we find that we are not given more help than we need in order to live there fruitfully. We can have all the help that we do need, but there is a limit to the help we can receive from anyone or any rule in our spiritual life, simply because that life is ultimately an affair between God and oneself, with all the unpredictability and infinite possibilities of a living relationship.

Because the cell is not just one place, it is a whole lot of places for us, perhaps it will help to have some idea of what we can expect from it, if it is the place where we are to be revived and find fruition. This one little room, that no one else will enter while you are the occupant, is equipped with everything necessary to minister to the solitude of the whole person; not to the social needs of the whole person as one of a family of Sisters who eat and work and praise God and receive the Sacraments together, but to the solitude of the whole person: body, mind and spirit.

William of St Thierry, the twelfth-century Cistercian, wrote a Letter (known as the *Golden Epistle*) to the Brethren of Mont Dieu, a Community of Carthusians, people whose life, unlike ours, was based almost exclusively on the cell. In this letter he related the theme of the cell to the progress of the spiritual life from its first beginnings to its consummation. In his treatment of this theme he used some metaphors that we might find helpful (thought not taken quite in the order in which he uses them).

Quite early on William describes the cell as 'a little heaven, devoted like the kingdom of heaven itself to leisure for the enjoyment of God'. *Vacare Deo, frui Deo*, to be empty for God in order to enjoy

God, he says: that is the purpose of the cell.[2] The bareness of the cell, its vacancy, is precisely that leisure, that space, that absence of things and people in which we are to hold intercourse with God alone. Our rule therefore describes the conditions in which this enjoyment of God is to take place: 'The cell shall always be kept clean and tidy, and its simplicity shall be recognised by the Sisters as a sign of their consecration. No one shall enter the cell of another ... '[3] You could not really have anything less calculated to stir the emotions, just a few little indications to stress the privacy and simplicity of the cell, a space always in readiness for the arrival of a Guest.

William calls it 'a Holy Place' which reminds us of the holy places of the Old Testament, the sanctuaries where the patriarchs had personal encounters with God and received great commissions from Him and experienced His intimate friendship. For us too the cell is a rendezvous place, a little sanctuary, and therefore to be regarded with reverence: 'The Sisters shall, therefore learn to regard their cell as a place where the Holy Spirit will reveal to them the mysteries of God and manifest to them the compassion and love of the Saviour'.[4] All this we accept with readiness and eagerness to grow into it.

But there is more to our actual experience of the cell than this. There are two ways in which the cell can become rather terrible and nauseating. It can only become like that through misuse, but it is a misuse to which we, in our disordered condition, are rather prone. For instance, we can misuse it as a place of selfish seclusion, to get physical comfort and to think about the things for which memory sets up a clamour as soon as we are on our own. But beyond a bare modicum, the cell has simply nothing to offer to us on these lines. It has nothing on which the animal human can feed.

---

[2] *De propentibus*, fol. 6r, col. A, line 31 to col. B, line 14. Latin version: J.-P. Migne, *Patrologia Latina*, vol. 184:314; English translation: *William of St Thierry, The Golden Epistle: A Letter to the Brethren at Mont Dieu*, trans. Theodore Berkeley OCSO, intro. J.-M. Déchanet OSB, Cistercian Fathers, 12 (Collegeville MN: Cistercian Publications, 1971), 21.

[3] *SLG Rule*, ch. 13.

[4] Ibid.

The cell can also be misused through presumption: it can be simply appropriated quite quietly as a place we are competent to occupy and make our own by filling it up with ourselves, marking with our individuality, not perhaps with actual things, but with our unconverted self. We can make it a continuation of the mental and even spiritual life we have led in the past, bringing everything that has sustained and consoled in the past into the present, refusing the poverty and the new, rather fragile life that the cell is offering us. However there is nothing in the cell that will feed or minister to a full self. There is the possibility of terrible self-deception here, but it probably would not go on for long because the result of a lack of willingness to start empty is that the cell becomes unendurable and you just have to get out.

William speaks of the cell as a prison for people in this condition; but getting out of it, he says, is not so much a matter of escaping as being rejected by the cell itself, expelled by its poverty and bareness. This is because it is the sphere of an element we have not learned to breathe, are perhaps not yet ready to learn to breathe. William says this:

> ... if we go into the cell under false pretences of any kind the cell disclaims us and casts us out. A holy place is not able to endure for long the carrion of dead affections or a man who is dead at heart. Therefore the cell quickly expels as an abortion the man who does not belong to it, it vomits him forth like useless and harmful food.[5]

That is putting it pretty strongly, but I expect we have all had some experience of being at one and the same time imprisoned by the cell and expelled by it. Even in the very short time that the common life insists gently that we shall be there.

William goes on: 'Admission to living with oneself is a matter for careful and prudent deliberation, for the man who lives with himself has with him only himself, such as he is. It is never safe for a bad man to live with himself', or for a sad man or an unbalanced man to live with himself: the modern world is full of people who cannot bear to be with themselves. Nevertheless, says William, 'man in the animal state [that is, people still living predominantly on the level of their

---

[5] William of St Thierry, *The Golden Epistle*, para. 146; trans. Berkeley, p. 22.

animal nature] may be admitted to the company of those who live in cells' (our Rule says that newcomers may have full entry into the enclosure) provided, he says, they are:

> ... humble and poor in spirit ... with the aim that they may become rational and spiritual ... Let them be received with all kindness and charity, borne with in all patience and indulgence.[6]

There is a beautiful passage in which William compares animal men (or beginners) to sparrows, inconstant, unstable, a nuisance, loquacious and addicted to pleasure; and rational men who are growing in the spirit to turtle-doves, 'in full possession of their manhood, with a spirit that is serious, chaste, sober, wearied of outward things and, as far as possible, recollecting itself within itself'.[7]

William neither despises the sparrow people nor does he expect too much of them. He is willing to find a place in the solitary life for both sparrows and turtle-doves and there is great encouragement in the beautiful and compassionate way he describes their respective progress.

So we are admitted to this life of the cell and we very quickly find we cannot really cope with it, and that is an excellent thing, a real start because, William says, the person who is still responding on the animal level of their nature —

> ... must be taught to look on his body as a sick person. For it is impossible for a man faithfully to fix his soul upon one thing who has not first perseveringly attached his body to one place. To try to escape ill-health of the soul by moving from place to place is like flying from one's shadow. Such a man as he flies from himself carries himself with him. He changes his place but not his soul. He finds himself the same everywhere he is, except that the constant movement itself makes him worse, just as a sick man is jolted when he is carried about. Sick indeed he should know that he is and he should give his attention to those diseased parts of himself in which his sickness lies. For the nature of his soul is not merely contaminated, but suffering

---

[6] *The Golden Epistle*, para. 146; trans. Berkeley, p. 59.
[7] *The Golden Epistle*, para. 188; trans. Berkeley, p. 75.

from serious infection, and it needs extensive treatment. Let him stay then without moving from his infirmary and continue in the course of treatment on which he has embarked until he feels himself to be cured. Your infirmary, you are sick and ailing, is your cell and the treatment which has begun to bring you healing is obedience.[8]

This is really very wise advice because it is something we can use. It is all very well being told the cell is heaven and a meeting-place with God when, in fact, our experience is anything but that. If, however, we are told that we are ill and that the cell is our infirmary, then that is more practical, because it enables us to go into the cell and remain there, not only in the right frame of mind but also in accordance with our needs. Everyone in the community is encountering God in a uniquely personal way: because we are all so different, and yet all set on the same thing, accepting that the cell may function as an infirmary acknowledges our frailty with humility.

Once we admit we are ill and need treatment, even if we are afraid of it, then the cell can do something for us. An infirmary is not just a place where you go because you are ill, but a place where you stay and get better. William connects this theme of sickness and the infirmary of the cell very closely to that of a spiritual director and confessor. Both the cell and the sacrament of penance have in common a great privacy and inviolability. So he says: 'Never be ashamed to show your ulcer, do not hide it.' Show it to the physician and then it can be healed. We are not to be interested in our illness but in getting well, and we heal by admitting our illness to God and letting Him see us.

The Rule tells us that in the cell the Holy Spirit will manifest to us the compassion and love of the Saviour, the Healer. That compassion is there for us in our sickness, and the kindness of God is primarily what we are going to find in the cell. So if the bareness and aloneness of the cell, instead of drawing out our longing for God, tends rather to bring up to the surface all the things that seem wrong, that should not make us unhappy or make us shun the cell. He has not led us into the wilderness to destroy us but to fill us with hope. All we have to

---

[8] *The Golden Epistle*, para. 188; trans. Berkeley, p. 97.

do is to be insistent in asking to be cured, patient and persevering under the treatment, 'The wounded surgeon plies the steel ... '.[9]

This is a lifetime's work, so the cell is not only an Infirmary, it is also, in another of William's metaphors, a workshop, a place of co-operation, 'demanding much hard work, much sweat. It depends on God's mercy and grace and on man's will and alacrity'.[10] All these good practices demand the cell as their workshop and an enduring perseverance in it.

This cell of ours, that we might experience first of all as a novelty in our lives, comes to be experienced as a prison, an infirmary, a place of conflict and of convalescence, a workshop, a sanctuary; all these things at different times. Through perseverance and stability we come to see it more and more as our natural base. In fact, to use a final image of William of St Thierry, as our rest. William, in what he says about sparrows and turtle-doves writes beautifully about the interaction of those who live in cells, whether sparrows or doves, and no-one is probably entirely one or the other. A stanza from St John of the Cross's *Spiritual Canticle* sums up:

> In solitude she bided,
> And in the solitude her nest she made:
> In solitude He guided
> His loved one through the shade
> Whose solitude the wound of love has made.[11]

That is what it comes to in the end: the cell was made, pierced for each one of us in the walls of the convent by the wound of love. Each cell is a nest in the crevice of the rock, a wound of love. It is from God himself that we have our solitary vocation and it is to Him that we look for the fruits of solitude.

———◆———

[9] T. S. Eliot, 'East Coker' from *The Four Quartets*.
[10] *The Golden Epistle*, para. 188; trans. Berkeley, p. 43.
[11] Mirabai Starr, ed., *Saint John of the Cross: Devotions, Prayers & Living Wisdom* (Boulder CO: Sounds True, 2008), 49.

THE JOURNEY
Sr Rosemary SLG

It is really too soon for me to try and write about my 'vocational journey'. True, I have been on this road for as long as I can remember,
but forty years in monastic life is barely a beginning. I am still discovering what it is really all about and, in a word, it is *astonishing*.

My childhood sense of astonishment at the extraordinariness of
being alive is at the root of it: it still overwhelms me. Indeed my earliest word for that was 'it', and 'itishness' meant the mood of ache
and longing brought on by beauty or solitude. We went to church on
Sundays so I learned at some point to identify this intense and
precious realization with 'God' and found in worship a channel to
release and enlarge it. I remember a moment at the back of the
cowshed at home during one Easter holiday when I said 'Yes' to God
quite specifically and consciously. I was about nine or ten.

The expectation of my parents and at school was for a girl to
have fun, get married as soon and as happily as she could, and have
wonderful children. All I learned about monastic life was in connection with the dissolution of the monasteries. Before I left school I
visited a Careers Advice Bureau who recommended that I become
a window dresser, because I enjoyed art and design and especially
life classes (so perhaps I should do something with people). Despite
this advice I did my best to opt for God and chose to train to teach
divinity. This gave me the chance to study in and beyond the
Christian tradition: in my fourth year of study for a B.Ed I immersed
myself in texts relating to the *via negativa* and was nourished especially by *The Cloud of Unknowing*, the *Bhagavadgita* and contact
with the local Buddhist society. Contemplative life was drawing me,
and I realised that it was not just going to happen by itself, I had to
do something about it.

I went to my college chaplain who twisted his dog collar and
wondered if he might be able to put me in contact with an abbot in
France whom he used to know. I wrote to Church House who sent

me information about the Church Army. Eventually in desperation I responded to a Roman Catholic advertisement that read,

Do you think you have A VOCATION?

Yes, I thought I had, but I was Church of England and did not want to become a Catholic. Nevertheless, the Vocation Sisters invited me to visit and sent me a package of leaflets that contained one about Fairacres. I warmed to what it said about a Carmelite ethos and mention of the writings of St John of the Cross. But I was not ready, yet, to investigate further. However, I rejoiced to learn that there are nuns in the Church of England and I admitted, at least to myself, that I had fallen in love with God and, astonishingly, some time in the future I would enter a convent.

The future came sooner than I expected: I had a challenging and exciting teaching post with students who were not much younger than myself, and I relished being in central London, but somehow it was just dust and ashes compared to the pull of religious life. When I read the typescript of a talk by Mother Mary Clare SLG I recognised in her someone who knew what 'it' was, who understood the ache and longing and stood at the gate of a whole life based on that reality. I took the plunge and visited Fairacres for a weekend, and things went on from there.

The biggest test was meeting the fierce and heart-broken opposition of my mother: how could I abandon her? I was her only child and my father had died only a few years previously. It was very hard for both of us, and only when she died in 1983 was I able to understand a little more clearly the pain of bereavement that I put her through. Sr Jane SLG said that if it was right for me it would be right for her too, but that it would take time. I began to learn how a vocation is not only—or primarily—for oneself; if it is real it is discipleship and a way of the cross.

Eventually, still in my early twenties, I came, and was astonished. For about the first twenty years I would even wake up each morning and think: 'This is extraordinary! What am I doing here?' In the struggle to arrive, I had hardly thought beyond being admitted as a postulant; I had thought of it as crossing a threshold into the beatific vision, so part of my immediate astonishment was how ordinary life went on. There was a bright red blanket on my bed, there was breakfast the next morning. I had looked forward to getting to know fellow novices and resolved that in community I would conquer my natural shyness, but relationships develop differently in silence and besides, almost everyone was twice my age. So I was lonely. And there was the Night Office at 2 a.m., so I was tired. And my prayer life dried up. For some the novitiate is a springtime of fresh insights and discoveries, for me there was the discovery of how much I was a child of the 1960s, formed by *Honest to God* and with a propensity for scepticism and ironic humour. At least, though, there was humour, and that helped. Looking back on the tears, the homesickness, and how often I fell asleep during prayer time, I do not regret those formative years. I was thrown back on God and I was learning to bear the side of vocation that is so much more God's work than ours.

Scraps of wisdom from earlier, tougher generations comforted me then, and still do:

> ... *plead to Him as the parched ground pleads*
>
> (Fr George Congreve SSJE)[1]
>
> ... *measure thy life by loss instead of gain*
>
> (Harriet Eleanor Baillie-Hamilton King)[2]
>
> ... *sit ye stone still at the feet of God*
>
> (*Ancrene Riwle*)[3]
>
> ... *in the deserts of the heart, let the healing fountain start.*
>
> (W. H. Auden)[4]

---

[1] *The Incarnation and the Religious Life: The Addresses Given at the Christmas Retreat of the Society of S. John the Evangelist, Oxford, 1879* (Oxford: Society of St John the Evangelist, 1930), 87.

[2] *Ugo Bassi's Sermon in the Hospital* (London: James Pott & Co. Ltd, 1885), 9.

[3] E. J. Dobson, ed., *The English Text of the Ancrene Riwle: Edited from British Museum Cotton MS. Cleopatra C.vi.*, Early English Text Society, 267 (Oxford: Oxford University Press, 1972), 398.

[4] 'In Memory of W. B. Yeats', from *Another Time* (London: Faber & Faber, 1940), 96.

And now? I am astonished at what the community has become, and how my expectations have changed over the years. I have witnessed many deaths, many new arrivals and various community projects; I have had to do a lot of growing up. There are fewer Sisters now, and we are older. It is hard, but salutary, to witness again and again the realities of aging, sickness and death, and astonishing to witness the daily miracle of community lived by such a diverse collection of people, and persevering. My initial longing and desire are undiminished and that, paradoxically, is a hunger that sustains me. I have both curiosity and detachment about the future. For me at the moment vocation is mostly about learning to see God in the ordinary and everyday, seeing through immediate complexities and difficulties; something that our Rule describes like this:

> ... by waiting upon God to be taught of God, both of the wonder of himself and of His will for the world, the intercessor will see that world in the light of God and, with compassion, will hold its suffering and lack of purpose to His love for healing and restoration.[5]

——◆——

---

[5] 'Intercession', *SLG Rule*, ch. 18.

So I surrender the social life,
In whose unquiet entanglements
I envied the Bedouins' distant calm,
The indifferent ease, and the shiftless tents.

So I escape with my proper pain,
Toting the sack of my sad, sick heart,
To find my desert, like Peter, and live
The still divorce of a life apart.

There I live, and there I sing,
In the mortal waste of a mortal bliss,
And the voice of the Baptist strings my soul,
Crying aloud in the wilderness.

Amado Nervo[6]

---

[6] Amado Nervo, *Poems of Faith & Doubt*, trans. John Gallas, Contemplative
Poetry, 1 (Oxford: SLG Press, 2021).

COMMUNITIES OF ANGLICAN NUNS IN THE UK (2021)

Benedictine Community of the Holy Cross (CHC)

Address: Holy Cross Convent, Highfields, Nottingham Road,
Costock, Loughborough LE12 6XE
Website: www.holycrosschc.org.uk
Email: sisters@holycrosschc.org.uk
Telephone: 01509 852761

Community of St Clare (OSC)

Address: St Mary's Convent, 178 Wroslyn Road, Freeland, Witney,
OX29 8AJ
Website: www.oscfreeland.co.uk
Email: community@oscfreeland.co.uk
Telephone: 01993 881225

Community of St Francis (CSF)

Website: www.franciscans.org.uk
Email: ministergeneralcsf@franciscans.org.uk

Addresses of houses:
The Community of St Francis, 2 Yukon Way, Leicester LE1 2AF
Email: leicestercsf@franciscans.org.uk
Telephone: 0116 253 9158

St Alphege Clergy House, Pocock Street, Southwark, London SE1 0BJ
Email: southwarkcsf@franciscans.org.uk
Telephone: 020 7928 8912

San Damiano, 38 Drury Street, Metheringham, Lincolnshire LN4 3EZ
Email: metheringhamcsf@franciscans.org.uk
Telephone: 01526 321115

Minister Provincial:
Telephone: 020 7928 7121
Email: ministercsf@franciscans.org.uk

Community of St John the Divine (CSJD)

Address: St John's House, 113 Coleshill Road, Marston Green,
Birmingham B37 7HT
Website: www.csjdivine.wordpress.com
Email: csjdivine@btconnect.com
Telephone: 0121 788 0391

Community of St Mary the Virgin (CSMV)

Address: St Mary's Convent, Wantage, Oxfordshire OX12 9AU
Website: www.csmv.co.uk
Email: guestwing@csmv.co.uk
Telephone: 01235 763141

Community of St Peter (CSP)

Address: St Peter's Convent, c/o St Columba's House, Maybury Hill,
Woking, Surrey GU22 8AB
Email: reverendmother@stpetersconvent.co.uk
Telephone: 01483 750739 (Mon–Thu, 9am–5pm)

Community of the Glorious Ascension (CGA)

Email: cgaprasada@gmail.com

Community of the Holy Name (CHN)

Address: Quarry Bank, Woodfield Lane, Hessle, E. Yorkshire
Website: www.comholyname.org
Email: bursarsofficechn@gmail.com
Telephone: 01482 770345

Community of the Sacred Passion (CSP)

Address: The Convent of the Sacred Passion, 22 Buckingham Road,
Shoreham-by-Sea, West Sussex, BN43 5UB
Email: communitysp@yahoo.co.uk
Telephone: 01273 453807

Community of the Sisters of the Church (CSC)

Website: www.sistersofthechurch.org
Email: info@sistersofthechurch.org.uk

Addresses of houses:
St Michael's Convent, Vicarage Way, Gerrards Cross, Bucks, SL9 8AT
Email for general enquiries: info@sistersofthechurch.org.uk
Telephone: 0330 120 0630

82 Ashley Road, Bristol BS6 5NT
Email: bristol@sistersofthechurch.org.uk
Telephone: 01179 413268

St Gabriel's, 27A Dial Hill Road, Clevedon, N. Somerset BS21 7HL
Email: clevedon@sistersofthechurch.org.uk
Telephone: 01275 544471

10 Furness Road, West Harrow, Middlesex HA2 0RL
Email: westharrow@sistersofthechurch.org.uk
Telephone: 020 8423 3780

Community of the Sisters of the Love of God (SLG)

Address: Convent of the Incarnation, Fairacres, Parker Street, Oxford
OX4 1TB
Website: www.slg.org.uk
Emails: sisters@slg.org.uk, guests@slg.org.uk
Telephone: 01865 721301

Order of St Benedict (OSB)

Community of St Mary at the Cross, Edgware
Address: Edgware Abbey, 94A Priory Field Drive, Edgware,
Middlesex HA8 9PZ
Website: www.edgwareabbey.org.uk
Email: info@edgwareabbey.org.uk or
nuns.osb.edgware@btconnect.com
Telephone: 020 8958 7868

Malling Abbey
Address: St Mary's Abbey, 52 Swan Street, West Malling, Kent
ME19 6JX
Website: www.mallingabbey.org
Community contact form: www.mallingabbey.org/bookings/en-
quiry.php
Telephone: 01732 843309

Order of St Benedict, Mucknell Abbey (OSB)

Address: Mucknell Abbey, Mucknell Farm Lane, Stoulton,
Worcestershire WR7 4RB
Website: www.mucknellabbey.org.uk
Email: abbot@mucknellabbey.org.uk
Telephone: 01905 345900

Order of the Holy Paraclete (OHP)

Website: www.ohpwhitby.org.uk
Email: ohppriorywhitby@btinternet.com
Telephone: 01947 899560

Main house:
St Hilda's Priory, Castle Road, Whitby, North Yorkshire, YO21 3SL

Other houses in the UK:
3 Acaster Lane, Bishopthorpe, York, N Yorks YO23 2SA
Telephone: 01904 777294
Email: ohpbishopthorpe@archbishopofyork.org

St Agnes Vicarage, 1 Broughton Avenue, Easterside, Middlesborough TS4 3PX
Email: sisteranita@btinternet.com

Sisters of Charity (SC)

Address: 15 Cornwood Road, Plympton, Plymouth PL7 1AL
Email: plymptonsisters@gmail.com
Telephone: 01752 336112

Sisters of Jesus' Way

Address: Redacre, 24 Abbey Road, West Kirby, Wirral, CH48 7EP
Website: www.redacre.org.uk
Email: sistersofjesusway@redacre.org.uk
Telephone: 0151 6258775

Society of All Saints Sisters of the Poor (ASSP)

Website: www.allsaintssistersofthepoor.org.uk
Email: leaderassp@socallss.co.uk
Telephone: 01865 249127

Main house:
All Saints, 15A Magdalen Road, Oxford OX4 1RW

Associated houses:
St John's Home (for elderly people), St Mary's Road, Oxford OX4 1QE
Website: www.accurocare.co.uk/
Email: admin@st_johns_home.org
Telephone: 01865 247725

Helen and Douglas House, 14a Magdalen Road, Oxford OX4 1RW
Website: www.helenanddouglas.org.uk
Email: admin@helenanddouglas.org.uk
Telephone: 01865 794749

The Porch, 139 Magdalen Road, Oxford OX4 1RL
Website: www.theporch.org.uk
Email: info@theporch.fsbusiness.co.uk
Telephone: 01865 728545

Society of Our Lady of the Isles (SOLI)

Address: Society of Our Lady of the Isles, Isle of Unst, Shetland
Website: sites.google.com/site/societyofourladyoftheisles

Society of St Margaret (SSM)

Hackney
Address: St Saviour's Priory, 18 Queensbridge Road, London E2 8NS
Website: www.stsaviourspriory.org.uk
Email: ssmpriory@stsaviourspriory.org.uk
Telephone: 020 7739 9976 (Sisters, except on Mondays); 020 7739 6775
(guest bookings)

Walsingham
Address: The Priory of Our Lady, Bridewell Street, Walsingham,
Norfolk NR22 6ED
Website: www.ssmwalsingham.moonfruit.com
Email: sisterangela@prioryofourlady.co.uk
Email for Bursar: bursar@prioryofourlady.co.uk
Email for Guest Sister: guests@prioryofourlady.co.uk
Telephone: 01328 821647 (admin); 01328 820340 (Sisters & guests)

Chiswick
Address: St Mary's Convent & Nursing Home, Burlington Lane,
Chiswick, London W4 2QE
Email: mother@stmarysnh.co.uk; maryclaressm@hotmail.co.uk
Telephone: 0208 994 4641

Society of the Precious Blood (SPB)

Address: Burnham Abbey, Lake End Road, Taplow, Maidenhead,
Berkshire SL6 0PW
Website: www.burnhamabbey.org
Email: burnhamabbey@btinternet.com
Prayer requests: intercessions@burnhamabbey.org
Hospitality: hospitality@burnhamabbey.org
Telephone: 01628 604080

Society of the Sacred Cross (SSC)

Address: Tymawr Convent, Lydart, Monmouth, Gwent NP25 4RN
Website: www.tymawrconvent.org
Email: community@tymawrconvent.com
Telephone: 01600 860244

Society of the Sisters of Bethany (SSB)

Address: 7 Nelson Road, Southsea, Hampshire PO5 2AR
Website: www.sistersofbethany.org.uk
Email: ssb@sistersofbethany.org.uk
Telephone: 02392 833498

Order of Companions of Martha and Mary:

Address: St Joseph's House of Prayer, New Vicarage, Church Lane,
Tunstall, Lancashire LA6 2RQ.
Website: www.companionsmarthamary.org.uk
Email: sistersocmm@gmail.com
Telephone: 03330 119563

SLG PRESS PUBLICATIONS

slgpress.co.uk